Thank You
for Being
a Friend

REVISED AND EXPANDED

Thank You
for Being
a Friend

My Personal Journey

JILL BRISCOE

MOODY PRESS
CHICAGO

ISBN: 0-8024-8547-2

1 3 5 7 9 10 8 6 4 2

Printed in the United States of America

Thank you for being a girl. You were a shock to your dad. He didn't believe he could produce one of our kind. I could see the bewilderment in his face as you lay snugly in his arms. "Whatever shall I do with one of these?" he asked me silently. You knew, didn't you. You knew that, man that he was from a man's world, he needed to learn what a woman was all about. Thank you for teaching him—*he's loved it.*

Thank you for being a tomboy. For falling off the donkey and joining in the football, and keeping up with every brother-step along the way. I tried to get you interested in dolls, but you just thumped your friends with them.

Thank you for coming to Christ. I can still see your sticky candy hands clutching at my baking board, your big blue eyes wondering if Jesus would want you to put your toys away if you let Him into your heart. I remember. Thank you for coming anyway even when I told you yes about the toys. Thank you for loving the Lord I love.

Thank you for loving Nanna like you do. I think you love her as much as I. How can that be? I really don't understand—but thank you for loving my mum.

Thank you for choosing the right friends. I just now see why you didn't choose the ones *I* chose for you. You were there on the right level. Thank you for choosing right. That was *very* important.

Thank you for wanting to please us, so hard and always. That was one thing we could depend on.

Thank you for telling me it was time for you to choose your own clothes. It wasn't worth a war—you taught me to keep the wars for bigger things . . . moral issues, questions of discipline—not for bits of cloth.

Thank you for yelling back at me when I got mad. You taught me that shouting did no good. Nothing got said that way. Screaming didn't settle things. We had to stop and *listen* to each other. Thank you for making me change.

Thank you for bringing me up right. No one else could teach me how to be a parent but you kids. And when I was afraid—thank you for taking me into my bedroom and sitting me on the bed and asking me what was the matter. You asked me if I trusted you and I said yes, but I didn't trust your judgment. Then you asked me how I expected you to develop judgment without experience. I told you my job was to know when you were ready for the experience—"Don't be afraid, Mum," you said—"I'm not." *That's why I am,* I said. Thank you for that and for teaching me I needn't have worried.

Thank you for challenging me with your discipline. For your running and your study habits, your bright mind you have determined to sharpen, train, and use for Him. Your fresh, sweet, unspoiled beauty catches my breath and turns it into thankfulness.

Thank you most of all *for being my friend.* For making me forget I'm over forty. For walking on the beach or in the mall with me. For slipping your arm through mine, even when your friends are there without their mothers. For giggling and saying—"I'm glad we're super close, Mum!" Can you possibly know what that's worth?

And thank you for coming to sing for me, for the way you have worked and played and traveled so many places. Thank you for all those fun times at the airport when you insisted on going to the ladies' room five minutes before it was time to board the plane.

And thank you for telling me you won't put me in a home when I'm old and alone—that I can come and live with you. (Although Dad wants to know what makes me think he's going first.) Incidentally, I won't ask that of you, Judy—but thank you anyway.

Thank you last of all for the privilege it's been to be your anchor, and for the confidence you've given us to "set your sail."

Yes, thank you for being a girl!

Contents

Preface   9

1. Shirley   11
2. Grace   25
3. Janet   39
4. Elspeth   57
5. Ann   75
6. Joan   99
7. Peggy   117
8. Angela   135
9. Mary   157
10. The Ultra-Suede Ladies   179
11. Prayer Friends   193
12. Judy   203

Preface

The heavens proclaim God's splendour,
    the sky speaks of his handiwork;
day after day takes up the tale,
    night after night makes him known;
their speech has never a word,
    not a sound for the ear,
and yet their message spreads the wide world over,
    their meaning carries to earth's end.
See, there is the sun's pavilion pitched!
He glows like a bridegroom leaving his chamber,
exults like a hero to run his course;
he sets out from one end of heaven,
    and round he passes to the other,
    missing nothing with his heat!
The Eternal's law is a sound law,
    reviving life;
the Eternal's is a trusty witness,
    that instructs the open-minded;
the Eternal's orders are just,
    a joy to the heart;

the Eternal's command is clear,
    a light to the mind;
the Eternal's faith is a clean faith,
    it will last for ever;
the Eternal's rulings are upright,
    and altogether just—
more to be prized than gold,
    than plenty of rare gold,
sweeter than honey itself,
    than honey from the comb.
Yes, and by them thy servant takes warning;
    in following them there is rich profit.
Yet who can detect his lapses?
    Absolve me from my faults unknown!
And hold thy servant back from wilful sins,
    from giving way to them.
Then blameless shall I be,
    from many a transgression free.
May the words of my mouth
    and the thoughts of my heart
    please thee, Eternal One,
    my strength and saviour.
                Psalm 19

Chapter One

Shirley

*B*ootle—gray and bleak, blitzed by the Hun—place of my birth. Who ever thought Bootle would be famous? The group with the "beat" that came from "Bootle"—the Beatles—lived there.

I was five, my sister eight when war was declared. I didn't understand what "war" was, but I learned to see hostility in the sky and to know enough to run and burrow underground like a mole. Some children have fairies at the bottom of their garden—we had a dugout, a place to go "just in case" we needed it. My father smiled reassuringly —"Just in case," he said again.

I remember looking at my sister. She was almost twice as big as I and certainly twice as beautiful. I think I decided then I could never ever be as lovely as she. Not that I envied her. I worshiped her! Even when my mother gave us two shiny new sixpences, saying, "Here you are, Shirley, one for you and one for Jill," and she lost mine, I didn't argue. If she said she'd lost mine she must know somehow—with some dark, clever, secret knowledge—that it was *mine* that was gone even though they were identical. Shirley was better than I, had longer thicker hair, bigger brighter eyes, and a very bossy voice. I loved her. If she told me we were playing shop, we played shop. And even when my five-year-old mind was tired, I obediently played shop until the last frock was sold and she decided it was closing time.

Day after four-year-old day, sitting curled and frilled, clean and cute, I waited on a little three-legged stool in our front yard till she came home from school. I didn't know anyone else went to her school, for who was so clever as Shirley? No one else could possibly have been so smart as to have passed the test to enter that august place of learning —so I sat on my little pedestal and dreamed about my clever sister, all alone in a big room with empty desks and one smiling teacher ticking all Shirley's sums right.

One day I left my perch and went to meet her. Surely her school was around the corner, I thought—hadn't I seen her disappear and reappear from there every day? But it wasn't just around the corner, so I wandered till I was lost. Shirley would find me, I told myself happily. Shirley would come and take my hand and bring me home. There was nothing in the whole wide world Shirley didn't know.

Shirley didn't find me, but a kind teacher did and asked my name. I lisped, "I'm Shirley's sister!" and I wasn't a bit surprised to see she wasn't a bit surprised. She knew who I meant, because everyone knew Shirley, of course.

I remember sitting on my stool in the front yard, gazing at the sky. I didn't know God rolled it out, then wrote things in clouds and sunset that a four-year-old could read. I didn't guess the crimson hues of seaside sunset spelled the character of God above. I didn't know the verse that says, "The heavens declare the glory of God; and the firmament sheweth his handiwork" (Psalm 19:1 KJV). But I remember the sky. I'd sit and stare and stare until my head ached, and then that frame of beauty would suddenly contain my sister's most loved face, and God was right there with me. Shirley was home.

But one day my little stool was put away in the corner of the kitchen, and my mother and Shirley were busy hanging up heavy curtains on the windows. They wouldn't let me sit and wait in the garden anymore, so I couldn't see the sky at dusk. My room was dark, unfriendly, shadowy, and somber. I peeked out the one small crack at my familiar sky and wondered why we had to shut it all away. I didn't know the sky was about to declare something else—this time not the glory of God, but the hostility of man.

They came—airplanes—from Germany. The airplanes carried bombs. Men drove them, opening the bellies of the black machines with the crooked crosses on the side so that big, black shadows fell screaming to the earth. My earth! They fell around my playground and my beach and my daddy's business and my sister's school. They were falling all over my life. They wanted to destroy my little three-legged stool and my mother's sewing machine and my sister's bike. And what could a little girl do? When you are five there is not a lot you can do but run down the garden into the dugout your father made and hope the bombs stop.

But they didn't stop. Night after night as darkness fell, Mother placed good warm slacks and jumpers nearby and we'd try to sleep. By dusk the sky declared a waiting world: searchlights and policemen; nurses caring for the previous night's wounded; old people crying—too tired to leave their beds again and take a ride outside the city walls to friendly meadows till the storm was past.

And we ran down the garden to the dugout. Where was God? And Jesus? Mother had told me They lived in heaven. Did They know about the war? Why didn't They lean over the edge and catch the bad men in the airplanes in midair? Did They care about my sister and me? Did They know we were in danger? I'd heard a grown-up say to my mother, "I hope my name is not on one of those bombs!" and I began to have nightmares about a black bomb with Shirley's and my names on it chasing us all over the world—a dream that reoccurred well into my teenage years.

Living in Bootle, in whose harbor were docked the British ships that provided food for the beleaguered nation, left us extremely vulnerable.

If I had ever read Psalm 19 I'd have asked a very relevant question at this point. How come the sky was not declaring the glory of God—but the hostility of man? Had God lost the war? As far as a little child could go, I asked the question anyway. I had begun to get the message. I had read the sky correctly; it had declared to me both the glory of

God and the hostility and evil of mankind. God and evil both were publicly, formally, and explicitly declared in my world.

Then one night it happened. Father called my mother from work and told her to be ready in a few hours to leave. We would be going to live in a safer place. I remember strong father arms and strong mother comfort cradling my little body in the back of a speeding car. But the thing that made me quite frantic inside was watching Shirley's small set mouth telling me she was upset at leaving behind all that was familiar and loved. We sped away from our house, away from Bootle and the bombs, away from the Hun and his hatred, from the sky full of exploding anger and the disintegration of somebody's son falling out of heaven to a foreign grave. We were safe.

I didn't know there were few places to run to in a country surrounded by sea—I didn't even know we were surrounded by sea. I was not aware that, in a land not much bigger than Tennessee, there was only so far to run—but run we did. We motored into God's country—the English Lake District. Running to the hills, calling on them to hide us, we stopped late at night, knocked on a tiny farmhouse door, and asked for shelter. A wonderfully kind farmer's wife cradled me up to a feather bed and "floated me" into its homey foam. They had no problems with the blackout as they had no electric light at all. Because of our common adversity, people cared for total strangers as if they were their own.

How quiet it was. How different the feather bed from our bunks in the earthen shelter, and, marvel of marvels, I could see the stars again. Vividly I recall the wonder of it all, the first "still point" of my five-year-old life. The war would stay in Bootle and we would live here forever, I thought. The night was my night, the sky was speaking, the heavens proclaimed their message, and their meaning spread my wide world over—indeed . . .

The heavens proclaim God's splendour, the sky speaks of his handiwork; day after day takes up the tale, night after night makes him known; their speech has never a word, not a sound for the ear, and yet their message spreads the wide world over, their meaning carries to earth's end. (Psalm 19:1–4)

Convinced the stars were holes in heaven, I gazed at "my book" about God so excellently propped open for me in the sky. It was *beautiful.* God was at home. I murmured, "Oh God, Your house must be so awfully bright for all that light to shine through."

God was without doubt a marvelously wonderful Maker of moons and stars and heavens and things like that. His handiwork declared it.

We rented a house, and Shirley and I started sitting on three-legged stools, losing our sixpences, and playing shop all over again. Our home had a small food service lift from the kitchen to the dining room above. This saved people running up and down stairs. It was fun to put the potatoes in the lift and shout up the shaft to Shirley to pull the load up. I would see it disappear with foreboding. *What would happen if my sister let go of the rope?* "It would drop on your head, silly," my mother remarked, pulling me out of the shaft.

I ran upstairs to see if Shirley was strong enough to deliver our dinner. I guiltily confided to her my doubts of her ability, and she turned and gazed at me with disdain. "As if I'd drop it! I'm strong. Get in," she commanded, "and I'll prove it!" I shivered. "Go on," she continued, "you'll see how strong I am. I'll let you down slowly, and Mother will get such a surprise seeing you appear instead of the dirty dishes."

I trusted her—of course. She was bound to hold the rope tightly, and it would be fun. I squeezed and scrunched into a knot and off I went—fast! *How could she do this to me?* I thought quickly as I hurtled toward the kitchen. It was the first time in my life Shirley wasn't strong enough and big enough and capable enough to support me. It was sort of a symbolic "dumping," for by the time I arrived in the kitchen—which, the law of gravity being what it is, didn't take very long at all—I had not only been physically let down but psychologically deposited as well. Shirley was devastated. She kissed me better, said she was so sorry, and I told her it was OK—but she had dropped me. I couldn't believe it. She wasn't God!

But if she weren't God, I still believed she was a pretty close relative. I needed her and she was there. In the next few years, she was to be my idol, and image of all I believed I was not.

* * *

My father was away and my mother kept a lonely vigil with thousands of other wives in wartime Britain. I never saw her cry. She made sure we were never lonely, so we thought nothing of her loneliness.

One Sunday, we played instead of going to church to learn about the God whom heaven declared. That day I discovered God doesn't live in a church-shaped box or a Sunday school room waiting to be visited by the faithful few. He'd *got out!* "Hide-and-seek—hide-and-seek—let's play hide-and-seek," I begged Shirley. "I'll hide and you seek," I said, and ran away—squeezing behind the big couch in the kitchen. No one saw me, no one found me. I'd done it; in the words of Christopher Robin, "Nobody knew I was there at all!"

Suddenly I discovered myself in another "still point." As if I were hanging in space and it were imperative, I answered a loud question. I couldn't see who was asking it—but I knew the answer was very, very important indeed. The question was "Do you really think no one can see you? What about God?" It was no good playing hide-and-seek with Him. There was definitely nowhere in the whole wide world I could hide where He would not see me. Feeling caught out, I emerged from my shelter and asked Shirley to read me a story instead.

One night I had a dream. I think it was a dream. There was a big field of sheep and I was standing in the middle. That's all. A field of sheep and me. I ran into my mother's room and told her about it. The thing that shattered me was that Shirley wasn't the shepherdess—I was. Somehow it didn't surprise me to be there—it was just as if I'd known that would happen one day—but oh, it did surprise me that Shirley wasn't with me and she wasn't responsible; I was! How could that be? Shirley was always responsible. She was so organized and capable and could count the sheep much better than I. My math was awful. Why wasn't *she* the shepherdess? My mother didn't know. But she listened and kissed me sweetly and told me Jesus loved me.

The war warred and we grew through four more years of sirens and food shortages and pictures of bananas we'd never tasted and shattered faces of amputated families. But we didn't have to run into a dugout anymore. It was nearly over. It was time to think about going home.

Shirley said she wouldn't go. She was so in love with God's country and her hosts of golden daffodils, she seriously considered leaving school and working so she could stay. Since she was only twelve, she had to comply with the family plans instead. Why go back to Bootle? What was left, anyway? Who of her friends were still living there, and why did we need to change from country to city living? I didn't really care where we lived as long as the sirens stopped and the shadows didn't fall from the sky.

Peace was declared—the end of hostilities was announced, good had triumphed over evil, God had won the war. I was nine and about to begin my race toward maturity.

Shirley was well ahead of me. She was absolutely beautiful. Long legs, black hair, and big brown eyes. She tanned deeply and quickly, while I was busy counting my freckles. She played a mean game of tennis, and the boys lined up along the courts applauding her play. Quite right too, I thought proudly. I began to be aware of many of the boys wanting to talk to me and believed it was because I might give them an "in" with my pretty sister. Why else would they want to talk to me? At that point I was not threatened by this thought; it was understandable, acceptable, and quite enjoyable. Bathing in reflected glory was better than no glory at all.

Shirley was sixteen—I, thirteen. In vain did my mother encourage me with such words as "You're just as pretty as Shirley—hold your head up high and look in the mirror and say, *I'm me and I'm fine!*" I did . . . that is, I looked in the mirror and, oh dear, the best I could manage was "I'm different! That's for sure."

"Your hair is an unusual color, Jill," Mother said.

"Yes, an unusual shade of 'mouse,'" I snapped back. Hunching my shoulders, I slouched about in a shape that said "excuse me for living." I began to withdraw into a dreamworld that helped me escape from reality. What reality? The reality that I was a freak! I was convinced of it. How could my friends bear to be with me? Even when boys began to ask me out, I attributed pity motives to them. So if I couldn't make it by being pretty, why not supplement my worth by being bad? That was something Shirley wasn't good at. I took off for long walks every night with a girlfriend. We sat in the park and talked with the boys—any boys—it didn't matter what they looked like, smelled like, or acted like.

Then Shirley found out what I was doing. She talked to me. She didn't want our parents upset. I listened—of course. But I didn't think she understood. I told her I would be good, and then I went on doing all the things she told me not to do. I figured that was the difference between Shirley and me: our parents trusted us both; Shirley proved their trust, I abused it. But then, I reasoned, my sister didn't have to do wild things to get the limelight.

I suddenly yearned to catch attention—anyone's attention. I practiced my tennis—winning two adult tournaments at fourteen years of age. Shirley hadn't done that, but I was still convinced she was a better tennis player than I. I practiced hard at my ice skating. I could do ten spins, Shirley could only do five—but she was old enough to skate in the ice show. We made her dress out of the pink "plastic" that had just hit the market, and I watched with insatiable longing as she and the other girls glided over the ice in the spotlights.

I decided to start a dramatic company. That was something Shirley hadn't done. I formed it one evening in the backyard with a few friends. I wrote the play in a day. It was about Miss Prune and Miss Prism and a wicked fairy and a sort of Cinderella (me, of course). I asked a friend to play her cello, and her sister announced our "variety act" before the serious stuff began. My best friend played a piano piece, and I played "They've Got an Awful Lot of Coffee in Brazil" on my recorder. We knocked on doors, hired the village hall, charged sixpence, and gave all the profit to charity.

Shirley and my mother didn't know about it, so they didn't come. I didn't invite them. The hall was filled (amazingly), and someone wrote about us in the paper, and then it was over—and a sense of loss enveloped me again. Shirley hadn't seen it. Why hadn't I asked her? I desperately wanted *her* applause, not the acclaim of a roomful of strangers.

What a strange child I was becoming. Mother and Shirley worried about me. If I couldn't be the way I wanted to be and couldn't be like my sister, I found I could be anyone I liked to be in my dreams. I learned to travel out of reality whenever I wished, to switch off and daydream through my days, leaving only one antenna up to field questions.

I began having nightmares and doing odd things. "Take the dog for a walk, please, Jill," said my mother. Dreamily taking the leash, I set off, stopping carefully at appropriate tree trunks. When I got back, my mother and the dog met me with justified consternation. It's not every day your daughter takes the leash for a walk!

"Take these crusts of bread up the road to Mrs. P. for her hens," my mother requested. I complied.

When I handed Mrs. P. the sack, she nearly dropped it. "For the hens?" she asked in a rather strange way, hauling a huge bag of potatoes inside the front door—I hadn't even noticed the difference in the weight.

"Bring me my slippers, Jill," my father requested. I disappeared. An hour later he asked, "Where are they?" I had no idea. We searched the house, eventually finding them perched neatly on the attic bed— an area of the house I'd not been near in years.

I was playing hide-and-seek again. This time I was hiding not only from Shirley, Mother, and Father, but from myself. If only I didn't need to be the me who lived in Liverpool and could be, instead, the me of my dreams.

But people kept coming to take me out of my fantasies and telling me I couldn't hide away like that.

Maybe the answer was to come out in the open and declare the game over. To do just exactly what my heart dictated, whether anyone liked it or not. Examining the ranks of the opposite sex, I decided to get me a boy. Mother didn't like him—neither did Shirley. That was a plus, I decided. He asked me to a dance. Taking a week to get ready, the day finally came. A bottle of very expensive perfume smiled at me from my mother's dresser. Opening it, I bathed freely. I did notice it was a bit strong, but surely the night air would dilute it. Hearing my father come home, I made my entrance poised precariously in my first high heels at the top of our long staircase. His attention caught not so much by the sight of me as the smell of me, my dad remarked, "Phew, doesn't she pong!" *That* didn't contribute to my self-confidence.

Floating toward and past him with my heart thumping, I wished with all my being that I didn't have to grow up at all. Taking my dog for a walk while I waited for my boyfriend, I ruminated on this sad state of affairs.

The sky was crystal clear, the stars, vivid in their beauty. I was young, strong, and free. Alive, well-off, and privileged beyond measure, I had everything—then why did I feel I possessed nothing? Who was I, anyway? I felt like a person living in a teenage suitcase that was locked tightly, taking me on a journey I didn't understand. It seemed as if people were slapping labels all over me trying to tell me where I was heading, and yet I didn't have any sense of direction myself.

I distinctly remember the next "still point." A Bible sat among my books. I had never opened it. I had never wanted to. Lying in bed one night, suspended again in time and eternity, an insatiable urge flooded me to open that Book and find out what life was all about, and what on earth I was supposed to be doing. The struggle ensued. I kept my hands tucked safely under the covers—I didn't reach out. I have wondered so many, many times where my eyes would have alighted if I had.

Perhaps I would have read that God had made me in His image, which made me a very important person indeed. Maybe I would have learned about the God who had only One Son whom He loved supremely even before heaven and earth were made and how He willingly sent Him to certain death for me. That would have given me a supreme sense of worth. Perhaps I would have read of "the Comforter," the Holy Spirit, One called alongside to help, and that He was available to succor me in my comfortless emptiness. Who knows what I would have read—but I didn't reach and I didn't read, so I didn't understand that God longed for me to know He never made an unimportant person.

Drowning in my inferiority, seeking to surface, I allowed my heart to become the "great dictator"—obeying its orders of a lifestyle contrary to that with which I had been raised.

If God was bothered about my behavior, surely He would be mad. Maybe the way to find out was to see if the sky fell on my head.

So I did, but it didn't. I got away with it! It wasn't that I didn't believe in God or didn't believe in being good, and it wasn't as if I didn't recognize wrongdoing—it was just that finding myself "unpunished from heaven," as it were, I came to a totally dangerous and quite wrong conclusion: God must have forgiven my transgression. I had not been struck down and my life didn't fall apart. Even though my "deliberate sins" were not in fact very bad at all, I knew if He was at all involved with the affairs of mice and men, they were serious enough to cause divine comment. When nothing drastic seems to happen as a result of actions we have been led to believe would cause God grave displeasure, then the obvious conclusion is that God doesn't mind at all.

My parents took Shirley and me to France. We toured the country. It was fun. We slept in the car in the French Alps one night. Trying in vain to get comfortable in the straight car seats, I gave up and wandered out to the edge of that delicious ridge of mountains. Dawn came. The sky was declaring the glory of God all over again. But what nature could not tell me were the moral things that, at that moment, I desperately needed to know.

When I looked at the sky I saw His majesty, power, and faithfulness. But I was only reading the sky, not the Scriptures, so His holiness was not being declared.

I ran to the car, fetched a pad and pencil, and—feeling poetic—penned a verse:

> *The dawn comes softly filling me with awe*
> *It seems the other side of Heaven's door*
> *That God forgives my sins to me is plain*
> *Each morning spite of sin—the sun doth rise again!*

If I had known Psalm 19, I would not have needed to pen another verse—the like had already been written. "Day after day takes up the tale, night after night makes him known." Scripture would have fully instructed me about God's moral law that I could not see in the stars or in the heavens—then and only then could I have known that I hadn't gotten away with it.

I would have come to understand that the fact the "sun doth rise again" when the sky should have fallen on my head did not mean that my sin had passed unnoticed and unjudged, but that God had graciously given me yet one more day to repent.

But Psalm 19 was Psalm 19. I was seeking more relevant instruction. At the time, life was too good to be morbid and religious. (I put the two together.)

And yet, in my celebration of life and in my seeking to find myself and do all my heart dictated, I still found the strangest emptiness imaginable. A new thought was gradually superimposing itself on my searching mind. A thought that didn't give me any confidence whatsoever: if God had seen my sin and hadn't done anything about it, maybe my actions had no consequence. And if my actions didn't matter, *I* didn't matter. That was the most dreadful thought that had ever occurred to me. If I didn't matter to God, then it didn't matter what I did or where I did it. I was of all persons most miserable. I began at that point to cease even to care to matter to myself. Without realizing it, the fact that I was important to my family and most especially to my sister had ceased to be enough. Somehow there had to be more. But more of what?

What confusion! I loved my sister and my sister loved me—and yet even our love could not release me to be me. I loved my selfishness while all the time despising myself and wishing I were not so. *Who was I? And why was I?* The early days of compliance, the complexes that followed the competition with my sister for love during my teen years had not provided me with that key.

It was time for the next "still point." It was time. It was time.

To Be a Friend:
Application and Journal

· ·

1. How has your childhood relationship with your sister affected today's relationship with her and with others? (If you don't have any
   sisters, think of your relationship with a brother or a childhood
   friend.) What habits or attitudes may have carried over: resentment or easy forgiveness, affection or distance, trust or caution,
   dominance or subservience, generosity or selfishness, teamwork or
   individualism, etc.?

2. What areas of your relationship have brought disillusionment or
   resentment, even bitterness? How has your role changed, for the
   better or the worse, to accommodate those areas?

3. Have you or your sister had the easier time getting others' attention? When has this been a battle, and how has that affected your relationship through the years?

4. What have you learned from your sister(s)?

. . . .

For Action:
Write a thank-you note to your sister, telling her your
appreciation for the good things you see in her.

. . . .

Chapter Two

....

Grace

....

$\mathcal{T}$he time had come to finish my education. There was an idea prevalent in Britain in my growing years that the way to "polish up" a girl after a good high school education was to send her to a finishing school. I had a few friends who were sent to such. They returned each vacation with every evidence of being polished "off"—not "up." *What was happening to them inside these mysterious European institutions?* Posture was improved and manners were acquired (or was it mannerisms?). How to make animated conversation about nothing very much could be an obvious plus for the cocktail circuit, but their faces reminded me of the display window in a jewelry store that had gone bankrupt: The window laden with all that the jeweler possessed, in front of an empty shop, gave a false impression to the casual passerby. Maybe I was being unfair in my judgment, but as I "passed by," I was not inspired to seek such an experience.

What was I going to do? I could leave school and get a job. Shirley had done that and was enjoying the freedom of being financially independent. If I went to college, it would mean dependence on my folks to see me through. And I had no idea what I wanted to be. On the other hand, college would allow me to start afresh. I could go to a place where no one knew me, leaving my teenage reputation behind, and have a chance to begin again. It was with such a lowly motive that I heeded a teacher's suggestion to apply to Homerton College in Cambridge to become a teacher. So my course was set.

The interview wasn't very alarming. I knew that although I was a mediocre student, I had been educated at one of the best private schools in England, and Homerton usually accepted one student each year from among the candidates from our school. Since I was the only one who applied that year, I was pretty confident of getting in.

I remember sitting in the waiting room with an extremely brainy-looking girl from another school district. She reminded me of a teacher I had suffered through who was brilliant but totally unable to communicate her knowledge. In trying to strike up a conversation with her, I wondered if all those advanced math, chemistry, and psychology courses and all her accumulation of credits had exhausted her time and capacity to grow in ordinary ways. Had she grown at all in such mundane directions, for example, as the tennis court, art festivals, world affairs, or even in the school of humor? I had a funny vision of her sitting in a Laurel and Hardy movie wondering why everyone was laughing. Imagine the poor children who would struggle with her boring psychology lectures on creativity!

If the interviewer was deciding between us, it all depended on what the school was looking for, I decided. Someone who didn't know much, but could teach it, or someone who knew nearly everything and couldn't.

I was soon to find the answer. I got the place. I certainly didn't know very much, but it was apparently apparent I had a natural ability to teach the little I knew effectively. The lady kindly suggested, however, that I concentrate in the preschool and first grade age levels—presumably working on the premise it's only necessary for the teacher to know a little more than her students.

And so I set my sail, packed my trunk, and boarded a train for Cambridge. I had never been there, had only seen pictures in books, listened to church music on Christmas Eve from Kings College Chapel, and read accounts in comparatively modern English literature about punts and the punted who fell in the River Cam. Sitting on the train, I wondered how it would all work out.

Soon I had to make a change, and there standing on the platform I saw another girl. Somehow she looked like me—all dressed up with somewhere to go. She was, I was sure, another new student. Her name was Sharon and yes, she was actually going to Cambridge and to Homerton.

She knew Princess Margaret, she said, and, oh yes, she did vacation on the Greek Islands. I noticed with admiration that she had blue, blue eyes, pretty wavy hair, and beautiful even teeth. After an hour's conversation, I reckoned she didn't know too much either, and I was glad she wasn't a brainy bore, but someone I could have fun with. Maybe we could room together? In fact, it was a friendship that was not to be, but meeting her relaxed some of my anxieties about college.

College was fabulous. I loved it all. The high, historic domes and castle-like bastions of learning. The narrow streets of Cambridge, shiny with rain and rough with cobbled tradition—snugly and neatly laid—paving the way for the feet of my new experiences. The triangular shapes of black-gowned male students riding bikes in the drizzle, with open umbrellas held aloft by strong and hairy arms, keeping their mortar boards dry. Where else but here, I wondered, could men look so foolish and yet look so right? It was a world apart. A society within a society.

In the safe confines of our women's institution, we sat at long misshapen tables. Each table was peppered with the women of tomorrow being made today. It was more than exciting to be part of such privilege. Briefly and inwardly, I thanked my mother and father for sending me here.

I decided to take the intellectually stretching courses like art and drama. I knew my limitations, felt I would fail at the "clever" things, and reckoned anyone could paint or be a clown. I have long since acquired a better appreciation of the gifts required for the arts. But feeling very inferior in the IQ aura pervading that atmosphere, I joined some extracurricular clubs that followed my bent and got busy living it up.

The drama scene looked good, and I became the property manager for a play. How humbly grateful I was for any small part that would bring me into social contact with such worldly-wise people. The students who ran the club were characters apart. If they just played themselves, I commented to myself, we would have an awfully good plot on our hands. The leader of the group was sleeping with his girlfriend, the makeup man confided to me. "Really," I replied—trying to make it sound as if I didn't need to be told.

It sounded fun, I thought. Sleeping with him, I mean. He was awfully good-looking. They asked me to their Saturday night party. I went. I was a little taken aback by the invitation. "Dress optional," it said in small letters in the corner. Small letters they were, but big in their impact. This was it! Here I was. This was "the outside world," and I was free to go—to try, to dare, to do or die. Here I had a choice no one else could make for me. I went to that party. I chose to go dressed. (Fortunately I couldn't stay long enough for the fun to begin, for I had to be back inside my college walls—my permit running out at a saving eleven o'clock curfew.)

How good of God to care for me when I didn't care enough to care! Strangely, I didn't resist those rigorous time limitations or even question them. Tradition reigned at Cambridge, and tradition taught that young ladies really didn't have the option to be out late enough to join in the "fun"—not in their first year, at any rate.

Cozy, underground, smoky wood-paneled coffee shops spattered the shopping centers. Swirling up the crooked stairs, curling around the corners, wisps of pipe haze informed one of tall, stall-like church pews cradling talking students. Boys met their girls and whiled away their leisure time debating undebatable issues. I soon learned the thing to do was listen. Any number of boys would gravitate toward the girl who did that. There weren't too many people listening in Cambridge. You either had something to say or you felt really out of it. But everything I listened to seemed to be a presentation of accumulated facts unrelated to a philosophy for realistic living. I didn't know there was a verse in God's Book that said some men were ever learning, but never coming to the knowledge of the Truth—but I did know the experience of listening to the "ever learners." There appeared to be a lot of people with a lot of knowledge, but seemingly they lacked the wisdom to know what to do with it.

Who was going to be the referee? Who was going to set himself up to blow the whistle on the foul play of scientific discovery being used to wrong ends? What man was there to say what was wrong anyway? Was a revolutionary a hero or a criminal? *It depended on whose side you were on,* I mused. But did it? Was there not a universal code of ethics everyone in the world could relate to, or did our culture dictate our behavior patterns?

I went to church. Just once. Looking back, my reaction was really quite sad—but I didn't feel sad at the time. The very first Sunday at college everyone seemed to be going. The bus stop was loaded with lines of girls looking nearly as self-righteous as I felt. Oh, how good I was! I tried to analyze why I was going and why I expected all the other girls at the bus stop to think I always went. Somehow I didn't suspect them of the same hypocrisy. Later I was to learn they didn't go either. Just the once. Just the first Sunday. Was it a sudden sense of a "past" for the first time in an eighteen-year-old's life? A leaving behind of the cocoon as we spread our wings in the warm, free sunlight of new maturity? Was it this that made us all feel vulnerable to the need of religion as a crutch?

Anyway, sitting still as could be in that ancient holiness, we wondered if anything could have been more aesthetically beautiful. Where could you go in the whole wide world to find the Kings College Chapel fare? The bell-like sounds of the white-robed people growing out of dark choir-pew pots, the windows like jigsawed rainbows, making people shaped in immobility move into your mind and tell the unsaid story of their doings. Hushed spirits of self-conscious students awkwardly leafing through an unfamiliar prayer book, sensing the "occasion of being" with a Holy Being. Somehow, in the quietness of my soul I felt a sadness. God must be terribly old. He seemed so couched in days gone by and therefore seemed to me to have lost His credibility with today's mad world.

Suddenly, as if the spell was broken, I joined the hysterical giggling of unchurched kids, trying to catch up with a curate trotting, nay, galloping us through a canticle. Up and down we went, when those who knew better were down and up. How embarrassed I felt. And why on earth should the vicar think such gymnastics would bring pleasure to God? No sooner was the kneeler knelt upon than the seat was to be sat upon, the incense put upon, and the offering opted on.

The huge Bible chained to eagles' wings upon a carved oak holder seemed incongruous. Not the Bible—the chain I mean. Just *who* did they think was going to steal it? I certainly wasn't, and I couldn't imagine any grubby thief taking off down a long dark Cambridge alley with a huge tome like that! No, the whole concept was medieval nonsense. The people who kept the chapel were obviously so cloistered they had become paranoid about their precious relics. It was all very picturesque and beautifully mystical, but certainly not intended to provide answers to the endless questions of our modern minds.

So ended for me my first and last college trip to church. The next week the line at the bus was noticeably shorter, and by the time a few more weeks had passed, the bus driver found himself alone.

Apparently my time at college was to be spent reading and learning about reading and learning. That was all. When I had contemplated the skies as a child and now when I speculated on the meaning of it all as a student, I came to the conclusion it just wasn't possible to know anything for sure. Answers were not to be found—just more and more questions, as if no one was qualified enough to say something in return. Where was the person who could have the last word to end this stream of searching agonies within me? I didn't know that the last Word had already been spoken when Christ was born. I didn't know. I didn't know!

Oh, Psalm 19—if only you had been written on the glossy pages of my teenage magazines! Then I would have known that "The Eternal's law is a sound law, reviving life" and that His Word makes wise the simple and enlightens the eyes. But instead Psalm 19 was written on the India-leaf pages of the Bible—a book that was definitely not on my reading list, but tightly chained through an antique lectern to its seemingly archaic past.

God's world had most surely declared His glory and majesty, but the problem was I had been looking at a spoiled creation that had not given me a true picture of the Creator, and the creatures of His creation in stately choir robes had not been talking or singing my language.

The time had come to stop my speculation of the Almighty from my three-legged-stool perspective, and begin to allow revelation from a more sturdy premise—that of the Word of God. But getting there was still in the future.

If God can't get you to a church that meets your need and He can't persuade you to open the written Word, He may bring it to you on two legs. I had never met such creatures before. In all my school days I couldn't remember anyone as religious as this. For now, among my college adjustments, I had to contend with sharing my very small room with someone who I was convinced was a religious maniac. She kept asking me if I knew where any other religious maniacs like her were. I gathered such people liked to get together and share their experiences—whatever that meant. I didn't know what she was talking about and, quite frankly, I didn't care. Elizabeth was a nice girl, and I liked her well enough, even though she seemed pretty holy. But I reckoned she must have had nuns in her family or something and just needed a bit of growing up at college to get it all out of her system.

One day she found out where they met. "They have a society and it's called 'KICK YOU,'" she chattered excitedly, not bothering to explain to me that C.I.C.C.U. (kick you) stood for Cambridge Inter-Collegiate Christian Union. I immediately equated it with the newscast I had been watching on TV the previous night. The horrifying news of the "Kikuyu rebels" in Kenya had just burst upon the world—and I certainly didn't want anything to do with that. It was funny, I thought to myself. I hadn't noticed any Africans around the school.

Elizabeth was not explaining God to me very clearly by what she said, but it didn't really matter because I was reading her lifestyle and getting the picture anyway. I couldn't help but notice the Bible loving-ly perused before she went to sleep, and I soon became embarrassingly conscious of the expletives she *didn't* say. She showed a sweet caring for my interests, and suddenly I was seeing the glory of God declared all over again. Not in creation this time, but in a creature of creation—Elizabeth.

The poem by Beatrice Cleland says it all—

Not only by the words you say, not only in your deeds confessed,
But in the most unconscious way is Christ expressed.
Is it a beatific smile, a holy light upon your brow?
Oh no! I felt His presence when you laughed just now.
For me, 'twas not the truth you taught . . . to you so clear, to me so dim,
But when you came to me, you brought a sense of Him.
And from your eyes He beckons me and from your lips His love is shed,
Till I lose sight of you and see the Christ instead.

Shortly after getting into the swing of things at college, I met an-other *living epistle* in my drama class. Her name was Grace. Little act-ing exercises were dispensed whereby we were expected to act out situations spontaneously. In one such exercise we were divided into two groups, then moved to opposite ends of the long room. Being a girls' college, our group was assigned to portray the male gender. We were supposed to approach our partner and strike up a conversation, as if we had seen her in the park and decided to "pick her up." Know-ing my partner was a living epistle, I maliciously enjoyed her discom-fort, for I was obviously embarrassing her. Without saying one word to me, Grace made me read my portion of the Bible for the day. Her attitude told me that such behavior was a stupid and unnecessary part of a lifestyle she did not care to emulate. Somehow without a word be-ing said, I knew her relationships were to be built on solid founda-tions, not on tinsel flirtations like mine.

Watching her furtively from that moment on, I was hardly sur-prised to hear her refuse a part in a play because of the four-letter words she would have to use. She began both to irritate and fascinate me, since I just couldn't seem to dismiss her quality of life as pious nonsense.

It wasn't that she didn't laugh; it was just that she appeared to possess a sense of humor from another planet. What was more, for someone with her head in the clouds, I noticed her feet were amazingly planted in college affairs at ground level. The day came when, to my absolute amazement, I discovered myself nominating her for the position of college president. Looking over the list of nominees, there was certainly no girl I disliked more, and yet I had no doubt that she was streets ahead of every other girl in the school. I was somewhere on that list too. Near the bottom of it to be sure, but on it. I was popular, but Grace was powerful. That was the difference.

As I think back, I can see her retracing her steps to the service line of the tennis court—her fine blonde hair casually but neatly dressed, bouncing on her slim shoulders. I remember asking myself how she always managed to look so maddeningly cool and fresh, when she must have been as hot and sticky as the rest of us. I think of the word "serenity" and at once I match it with her name. Always unruffled, I sensed she would have something important to say if she needed. I thought how nice it would be to send her to the home of a friend who had just had someone drop dead. I couldn't imagine her shuffling her feet and casting around for irrelevant inanities. She wouldn't push the panic button and run. I had never opened the hymn book that contained that verse—

> Drop Thy still dews of quietness,
>   Till all our strivings cease;
> Take from our souls the strain and stress,
>   And let our ordered lives confess
> The beauty of Thy peace.

—but Grace's serene attitude sang it to me anyway.

I grudgingly acknowledged the fact that she encouraged visitors from overseas to "buy British," and I took note that she was *really*

English without laboring the nationalistic thing. She dressed impeccably in English tweed or whatever the occasion demanded. I never saw her clothes say anything wrong. I remember my mother telling me the art of dressing well lay in choosing the right attire for the right occasion, but I was not so favored with a natural taste for line and color. Grace's good dress sense made me feel like someone putting the cutlery all in the wrong place for an important meal. It wasn't that I didn't have the right clothes; I was just somehow lacking innate discernment of when to place them where.

I wondered what it was that gave her that infuriating composure. Was it some hereditary advantage the elite of England's upper class enjoyed as birthright? What was it, oh, what was it, that set her so apart? How I wanted to "quality" everything I touched as she did.

But being around her made me feel rather shabby and raw. I caught myself beginning to need to justify my beliefs; and that wasn't easy, since I had very few indeed to justify. I had a distinct feeling that Grace was reading me like a book and couldn't wait to finish it and start on something more interesting. I decided that the best thing to do was keep out of her way, but that was easier said than done. Like a small child brought firmly back to the pages of her homework, God made sure I got to read my portion of His Living Word every day. It seemed she was always around.

Then it happened. One of my professors asked me to take a note to her room. Racing up three long flights of stairs, I thumped along the corridor noisily, whistling and leaping the lines on the floor. Reaching her door, I knocked briefly and, without waiting for a reply, barged straight into her room. Grace looked up. She looked up because she was down. Down on her knees with her face to the Rising Son—saying, "Lord have mercy on me!"

I will never forget to my dying day what I felt like. I will never forget because I had been there before. I was back in my "still point," but this time it seemed to last an eternity. God was there, Grace was there, and I was there. Suddenly, frightened and vulnerable, I recognized His Presence and wanted to cry.

The girl who knelt at the side of her bed stayed there. She didn't leap up embarrassed at being caught praying in this day and age, and she didn't continue her heavenly intercourse and ignore my crude interruption either. She just smiled—and—

Was it a beatific smile, a holy light upon her brow?
Oh no! I felt His Presence when she smiled just now!

Suddenly, the "still point" was over and anger arose in my heart. How could she make me feel like this, hesitant, stupid, and lost? I had just begun to gain some outward confidence—how dare she make me feel so unsure of myself all over again? Throwing the note down on her bed, I literally stamped out of the room. The next few hours, I sat in lectures, concentrating very hard on forgetting my stupid and immature reaction and wondering, *Why, oh, why did I feel so jealous?* Why was it that I couldn't bear to think of the exquisite sight of a lovely girl bent in adoration—in tune with reality—at peace with herself? Was the raw fact of the matter that I couldn't stand to think of it because I wanted all of that too? Grace didn't have to be compliant to someone more dominant than herself. She was free from complexes because God had somehow relieved her of the necessity to compete. She hadn't needed to down anyone and everyone, to win out on top and be recognized. She had it all.

My anger was totally unreasonable. *Why should she be God's favorite child?* I asked myself reluctantly. Why should they have such a good thing going when I didn't have anything going at all? In the days that followed, I had an almost irresistible urge to creep back upstairs and peep through her keyhole to see if they were still at it—God and she.

I had read my Bible lesson, and what a lesson it had been! All Grace's peace of mind, glad attitudes, and able service were linked to that kneeling position by her bedside, and now I knew it. I thought maybe that was what was making me so angry. It was as if I had discovered some secret weapon, some mean advantage she had over the rest of us. No wonder she was elected president—she had resources denied to us mere mortals. Someone ought to expose the whole scandal. But how did you get the school magazine to print a story about our new president's hidden Friend? I was suffering from plain bedrock jealousy, that was all, tired out from trying and never quite making it, and oh, so homesick for a touch on my thirsty spirit of that "Still Point Presence."

I decided to check out Grace's male friends and see if they were as infuriatingly interesting as she. I was sure they would be strange, monklike creatures with wild, sad eyes, sneaking contemplatively around, thinking about all they had missed out on in life. I imagined them mouthing tuneless anthems and endlessly visiting the sick who were sick of being endlessly visited. But I discovered that Grace's friends were the most athletic, gorgeous hunks of men around. Her boyfriend was, in fact, to become captain of England's cricket team. They were the sort of men I always dreamed I would meet at the next party but never did. Were God's favorites indeed the best and not the worst specimens of male society?

I had to catch them out. They couldn't be as good as they looked. If I could just get close enough, I was sure I'd find some blemishes, and then I could dismiss the whole thing.

In the days that followed, I did get close enough to see the blemishes, but I found I simply could not dismiss the whole thing, for I had read enough of those living epistles to make me want to read more. I had seen God in nature, and now in human nature, but even that was not enough. The problem was, both were marred. Even Grace was Grace and not Jesus Christ—and, though I had seen God declared in His world and now in a woman, I had not yet seen Him perfectly. It was time to see Him in His Word. It was the Law of the Lord that was perfect, according to my unread psalm, and it was that perfect law that God would use to convert my soul.

To Be a Friend:
Application and Journal

. . . .

1. Sticking with people you know personally, name as many people as you can whom you admire. Why do you admire them?

Person   **Reason for Admiration**

_____   _____

_____   _____

_____   _____

_____   _____

_____   _____

_____   _____

_____   _____

2. Which traits above do you see as your own strengths? Weaknesses? What traits would you like to be remembered for (whether or not you are currently strong in those areas)?

3. Which people in the list above do you consider friends? Are there other people you would like to have as friends? What are the obstacles to such relationships becoming friendships? Are those obstacles real or imagined?

4. What fears are most likely to hinder you when you are entering a potential friendship?

. . . .
For Action:
Call one person from your list and thank her for the positive influence she has had on you. If possible, invite her to lunch and thank her in person.
. . . .

Chapter Three

....

Janet

....

Have you ever been in hospital before?" inquired the pretty young nurse as she wheeled me on the long trolley around a green corner of the hospital corridor. "No," I replied carefully. I was glad she had asked. I thought that if she saw I was new at it, I might get some preferential treatment, which was all right with me.

Addenbrooks Hospital was a teaching hospital, I was informed. "Oh good," I said weakly, panicking inside. Not only was I new at it, so were they. Nothing more was said, so I turned my attention to my new surroundings. I hoped I could stay on the trolley a long time. Being wheeled around like that gave me a false sense of going somewhere. It put off the evil moment when they would neatly package me for healing and lay me to rest. That thought of "permanence" in this austere institution frightened me. I told myself I had been very lucky to have arrived at the grand old age of eighteen before having a spell in a hospital. I decided it must just be the fear of the unknown that was haunting me—which was sure to pass as soon as I got acclimated. I had heard the food would be steamed tasteless, and I had anticipated that the nurses' uniforms would remind me of starched ship sails, but the thing that took me by surprise was how very small I felt and how totally unprepared I seemed to be for this unexpected venture into healing's halls. I had a ridiculous impulse to ask the nurse to "kiss it better"—like my mother used to do for me when I bumped my head—and let me go home.

Passing another trolley in the hallway, I tried not to look. I was sure the poor man on it was as embarrassed as I. I wasn't used to seeing people in their nightshirts, and apparently neither was he. He gave me a conspiratorial nod of his head as if to say, "Excuse me for dressing like this, but I really had no option"—and then he was gone. The moment was really awkward, as it seemed to strip him of his respectability, making him look vulnerable and foolish. There was something else. To be wheeled about when I could perfectly well walk seemed somehow to be the first demoralizing step in a process that gave me the rather frightening, foolish feeling of having become a senior citizen. Being a mere eighteen years of age, I'd not even gotten used to the idea of being a junior citizen. Just the act of that hospital blanket being tucked around me reminded me of Grandmother's arthritis, hot water bottles, and wrinkles.

I began to think about the pain that had brought me to this place. It hadn't gone away. Attacking me suddenly, without any warning at all, it would arrive in the middle of a lecture or at mealtime, or even in the dead of night, jerking me into a quick bending movement of self-defense. Being inordinately fond of myself, I made sure people around me knew all about it. I mean *all* about it—all the details that obsessed me as soon as the pain possessed me. But no one seemed to know how to cure it. Lying on the trolley, being wheeled down corridors that appeared to go nowhere, passing efficient, briskly trotting nurses going determinedly somewhere, I felt a certain relief that someone was going to get to the bottom of the problem.

A young intern in a stiff white coat entered the reception room where I was temporarily deposited and smiled at me reassuringly. He produced some forms and began to ask me questions. They gave me a sense of importance, being queries about my past general health. How nice it was that these good people wanted to know so much about me. The kindly interrogation took my mind off the big pain and assured me someone cared.

Down toward the bottom of the page, the young doctor came to a question that stymied me. "Religion?" he asked. That was all. *Religion? What did he mean, and what should I say?* Church of England? After all, everyone in England was Church of England, wasn't he? Hadn't I gone to a school where the Creed or the Book of Common Prayer was used every day? But then I had never actually gone to the Church of England—unless you could count my first and last visit to Kings College Chapel. Did one visit give me something to say when I was asked, "Religion?" Would that do?

From somewhere deep inside of me I seemed to hear the question "Would it do what?" "Well," I answered the voice impatiently, "it would do enough!" Enough to let me state I had a religion. Everyone ought to have a religion, I mused. It was like having had measles or chicken pox as a child. It was one of those rather unpleasant things you felt you *should* have in your past as part of your growing up experience to prove you were just as normal as everybody else. But somehow I couldn't tell him to write Church of England on that line. It didn't seem really honest to say it.

Well, I thought quickly as the nurse assisting the physician gave me a curious glance—wondering, no doubt, why I was taking so long to come up with an answer—*I'd better put something down.* I decided simply to say "Christian." So that's what I did. After all, I said to that annoying inner questioner, I wasn't a Buddhist or Mormon or pagan, was I? I reasoned that England being a Christian country and myself being a citizen of England meant that that's what I must be. I was, of course, confusing the word "Christian" with "Western"—but I didn't know that then. Without any reaction, the crisp young man scribbled in my response, got to his feet, smiled knowingly about something he didn't care to divulge, and took his leave.

Finishing off the form meant my time in the reception area was over. The sister in charge was to assign me a place. The hour had come to take up frightening permanence in a ward. A ward was one huge bedroom containing twenty or so patients. You could only see the heads of the victims, their bodies having been laid in somber macabre stillness between white bed sheets that reminded me of tarpaulins battened down as if for burial at sea. Two nurses rolled me off the trolley into bed and similarly tightened down my sheets until I was in strait-jacketed conformity with the rest of my fellow sufferers.

I was soon to understand exactly what the word "ward" meant. Meeting Sister gave me the clue; I wondered which prison had given her leave of absence. She terrified all of us, patients and nurses alike. The first thing I learned was how to prepare for the doctors' rounds. Rounds meant an hour of preparation for the patients. If we didn't need a doctor before the rounds, we surely did by the time they came. We were scrubbed, shined, and polished along with the floors, lockers, and entire ward. Our bedside cupboards had to be placed in strict precision in line with our bed heads. Nothing was allowed to be out of place or left on top of our lockers during rounds. No piece of the body was even permitted outside the bedclothes. If Sister could have put us in the cupboards along with our untidy belongings, I'm sure she would have done so.

Our Sister was surely the fiercest old battle-ax we had ever had the misfortune to meet. Someone whispered (we weren't allowed to speak during rounds) that she had been jilted as a young lady. I mentally took off my hat to the young man who had had the courage, and I wondered where his grave was.

It was not too surprising that the doctors' rounds were expedited very quickly. The poor men must have been dizzy as Sister flitted them around the room and out the door again in short shrift. No patient dared to ask a doctor a question, by Sister's command. That just wasn't to be done on *her* ward. Even if you were dying to inquire how long you might have left upon the earth so you might put your house in order, Sister hovered in the background looking like a praying mantis and made it abundantly clear: it would be a very short period of time indeed, if you dared to pop the question. It was as if any query would be a reflection on her tender loving care for us and would put her in a bad light. She was obviously determined that the doctors should note that *her* patients had no questions—proving they were totally satisfied with the hospital at large and her in particular.

I noticed that a temperature chart had been hung at the end of

each of our beds. It went without saying that we were not to look at it
—even though every Tom, Dick, and Harry from paperboy to electri-
cian who walked past was apparently free to read the inside story of
our sufferings, graphically portrayed in funny dotted mountain peaks.
Finding me hanging upside down over the end of the bed, seeking to
find some answers to my unasked questions, the Praying Mantis (as
she was now fondly called at my suggestion) pounced on me and
slashingly reduced me to a quivering heap among my pillows. Taking
my temperature just ten minutes later, a sympathetic nurse observed
the chart didn't stretch far enough to record the Everest elevation her
attack had engendered.

Most of the nurses were great. We decided, however, that one
named Maureen must be related to the Mantis. In fact, we could have
called her the Black Widow. She was the worst nurse possible—bad
tempered, clumsily loud, and unkind. We dreaded her turn of duty.
Late one night when she was at her grumpiest, I was awakened by the
girl in the next bed weakly telling her she did not want a hot water
bottle. Having just come back from extremely painful back surgery,
she was running a fever and certainly didn't need any extra heat. The
Black Widow snapped at her, *Since she had asked for it, she would jolly
well have it,* seeing the nurse had taken the trouble to fill and fetch it
for her. Plunking the very hot bottle in the poor girl's bed, she
tramped off down the ward.

I was furious and, hearing a small sigh in the dark (there was no
strength left for anything more), I asked, "Do you want me to take it
off you?"

"No thank you, Jill," the voice replied softly, "I don't want you
getting out of bed. It's all right—it's all right." *How did she know my
name?* I wondered. But then I realized I knew hers—I'd listened to the
nurses giving her post-operative help and heard them call her Janet.

Why did she remind me so of Grace? Grace was five feet seven
inches, slim, blonde, and graceful, while Janet was small and dark. It
must be her eyes, I decided. They had that same translucent quality, as
if something was lighting up her life from the inside.

In the days that followed we became friends. And I was getting better—though my mysterious pain had not yet been identified. It was occurring at less frequent intervals, so I could sit up a little and talk to other patients to while away the time. I found Janet great company. She was a lovely girl and a good listener, which suited me fine, as I was a good talker. I discovered she was a nurse. Actually a sister. She had hurt her back lifting patients and had had a series of painful operations, fusing the bones of her lower spine together. She lived outside London, possessed a terrific sense of humor, and was very happy. All the time. That was weird! She actually radiated contentment, even when her back was very painful. It was as if she knew something I didn't know and was excitedly savoring her secret. I had the strangest sense of anticipation, being aware, somehow, she was getting ready to share whatever it was with me.

Just as I was beginning to relax and really enjoy her company, it happened. Chattering on about everything and everyone as was my wont, I happened to mention that I had had trouble filling in the hospital entrance forms. "There was the strangest question on that form," I commented. "It asked me what religion I was. I put down Christian!"

Puckishly I glanced at her, expecting to hear her giggle along with me at my clever sidestepping of the issue. Instead, she calmly and coolly looked me straight in the eye and asked me the thousand-dollar question—"Are you, then, Jill? Are you a Christian?"

"Of course, who isn't?" I shot back.

"You isn't, I think," she said with a laugh. I was secretly hurt. Who did she think she was? Was she saying she was a Christian and I wasn't? Was she implying I was dirty, or rotten, or an alcoholic—or something?

Seeing my face, Janet hastily fished in her bag, which was hanging on the bedpost. I watched her, not wanting even to help her struggle to reach it from her position flat on her back in bed. I suppose my callous attitude stemmed from the fact she had just metaphorically put me flat on *my* back.

Having achieved her objective, she handed me a little booklet that was simply entitled "Becoming a Christian." She smiled encouragingly. Taken aback and not a little puzzled, I thanked her and clambered back into bed again, wondering how I could become something I already was. It was all very confusing. As I lay suspiciously eyeing that unopened booklet, I glanced across at Janet. I was glad I was in bed. Otherwise I might have fallen clean over backward. She was reading a Bible! Yes, yes, a real live Bible. It had a red cover and seemed preposterously large. Glancing over at me, she must have mentally added another fact to her assessment of my character. The night I was admitted she had summed up my state of mind as eighteen and frightened. Now she added eighteen, confused, and not a little angry.

But why was I so angry? Was it because I had just been able to get to know this neat girl and was beginning to enjoy her friendship . . . and now I suddenly felt shut out behind that tantalizing book cover? Or was it because I felt somehow betrayed—for I found myself entertaining the ridiculous notion that Grace had planted her next to me in Addenbrooks Hospital just to get to me about religion.

There was absolutely no doubt in my mind that Grace and Janet belonged together. Theirs was a kinship I instantly recognized. Almost a "smell"—as if a sweet, sweet fragrance of the Spirit intoxicated me—making me long to know more about Him. This time I couldn't slam the door and run away embarrassed from the sight of another girl enjoying this strange secret Friendship I knew nothing about. I had all the time in the world to watch and think—and read. Dare I? Would I? Lying there, looking at that little blue booklet with the red lettering on the outside, I seemed to remember that night, long ago, in Liverpool, when I was inwardly urged to open that Bible by my bedside. Amazingly, all those years later, I resisted again and fell instead into a troubled sleep.

The next day, during our rubber chicken dinner, Janet asked me if I had read the booklet. "Yes," I lied casually.

"Did you do it?" she asked next.

"Yes," I lied again, not having the faintest idea what she was talking about.

"Oh, Jill, that's simply marvelous!" she exclaimed. I asked her to wait a moment, and I reached hastily for the little booklet, beginning to read it through as though I wanted to refresh my memory. I observed that it was written by a Church of England vicar. So it must be all right. Janet interrupted my reading excitedly to ask me—"Do you fully understand, Jill?"

"No," I stammered, "I really don't. Tell me what it means, Janet."

She snatched the book out of my hand and fumbled for her Bible in her purse. I wished she hadn't done that. Just the sight of it made me feel awkward. *Who was watching?* I wondered. *What on earth would they think if they saw Janet reading to me from a Bible?* They would think I was a prostitute or something! But somehow my curiosity and searching heart enabled me to ignore the curious inquiring eyes of my fellow patients.

Janet was talking about sin. *What a strange old-fashioned word to use,* I thought. It reminded me of the times I went ice skating and stayed to watch my favorite hockey team scamper about the rink chasing that elusive puck. When one or another clobbered someone with his hockey stick, he was sent to the "sin bin" as a penalty. The offender had to stay there till the penalty had been paid. I recounted this to Janet, and she said, "Well, that's how it is with us, Jill—we fouled out and we are all in the sin bin."

"All?" I asked. "You too—and Grace? Who's all?"

"All is you and me and everybody else," she answered. "Who's Grace anyway?"

"Don't you know?" I asked incredulously. "I thought you two must be relatives." Before I could stop myself, I poured out my story about Grace and how I loved, yet hated her for her secret friendship with a God I didn't know or understand at all.

Janet smiled an excited, private smile. I know now she was thrilling to the fact that God had been there before her—"there" being my heart and mind and prepared, receptive spirit. "There" being a highway made in my life, making way for her King.

She explained that the whole world had fouled out—some had simply fouled out sooner than others. But there wasn't one single human being on the face of the earth who wasn't sitting in God's "sin bin," condemned for breaking at least one of His rules.

Drawing me back to that little book, she gently led me through it, explaining as if to a small child the story I seemed to have been created to hear. I knew how Christ had died, but *why* He died I'd never been able to figure out. She explained He did it to take the penalty for our sin, so we could be forgiven and play the game of life with a whole new beginning. "He wants to wipe the slate clean, and He will if we ask Him to," she told me.

I didn't know about all those verses between the morocco covers of the King James Bible that talked of cool waters to a thirsty soul and a spirit that hungered after rightness—but when she told me that it was possible to have a fresh start, it was as if I suddenly became aware of how dirty I was and how it had become necessary for me to plunge beneath the water of forgiveness and never surface again. I didn't even know till that moment how desperately I wanted and needed to be clean inside. "The Eternal's faith is a clean faith, it will last for ever," said my unread Psalm 19. I felt as if I were perched precariously on the end of a diving board and hardly dared to let go, lest I hit concrete instead of water and be shattered into little pieces of disappointment.

"Jesus is alive," Janet told me quietly. I didn't doubt her—lost in the biggest still point of all, I knew it to be true. "He wants to come into your heart, Jill." *Yes, yes,* my hungry heart screamed. It was thudding with a "boom" I believed the whole hospital must hear, but Janet couldn't seem to hear it. Feeling sick with a giddy apprehension, I knew she was about to take me over the line that had separated me from her and from Grace, from Elizabeth and from all those other sisters of love I was yet to meet. I didn't know what to do, so I just sat still with longing, hoping she'd see my plight and somehow help.

"Do you want Jesus, Jill?" she whispered.

"Oh, Janet, yes—but I don't know how." The tears came then. How stupid I felt, for even though I sensed this was undoubtedly what I had been searching for, I just didn't know how to connect.

"I'll help you," Janet was saying. "I'll pray a prayer and you can pray it inside of you." Shutting her eyes, she took my hand and led me to her invisible Christ. "Jesus," she said, praying in the first person, "please forgive my sin. Thank You for taking the penalty for it. Come into my life now because I really need You. Live in me—be my Friend. Amen."

I repeated it after her with my whole being. Yea, I said it, sung it, shouted it to heaven. Jesus. Jesus Savior! It was done. It was over. He was there. Wonderingly, we looked at each other—

Suddenly, the spiritual aura was splintered by Sister's staccato voice snapping, "Into bed everyone. Visitors!" Lying in my parade position between my sheets as the nurses bustled around me, I thought about what had just taken place. I had no way of knowing all that lay ahead. Blessed amnesia! How good of God to veil the future. But I did have the ability to look back and think of all that lay behind. I thought of my struggle to compete with my contemporaries for boyfriends or popularity or tennis trophies or skating prizes. All my life I'd been trying to prove something to somebody. And now God had proved something to me. I didn't have to offer some prize for His friendship. He would be my Friend, as if He had no other. I didn't need to compete for attention—I had His undivided care. I didn't even need to win at something to feel a sense of worth. I knew Christ thought me worth loving *in spite of* not *because of* anything I did or said or tried to be. Suddenly, a tight coil seemed to unwind inside of me, and I was at peace, it seemed, for the very first time in my life.

I thought of the boys I knew. Most of them had lived by a philosophy that said, "I'll love you if you are pretty," or "I'll love you if you're fun to be with"—or even "I'll love you if you let me." Conditions needed to be fulfilled to win their love. But then I had had my conditions too. Conditions such as "I'll love you if you're handsome"—or "I'll love you if you've got a sports car to take me around in"—or "I'll love you if you have money to spend on me."

What a weird sensation to know someone would love me with all of my shortcomings and uglinesses and shallow selfishness. Now I could stop pretending I had something to offer that I wasn't even sure I possessed. Understanding me better than I understood myself, He still desired to live within my heart, knowing I had no earthly currency to buy His love.

I mean, "a cat can smile at a king," as the saying goes. What could I possibly have that God could want or need? No, He loved me, knowing full well the bankrupt vaults of my life, and I could rest in that knowledge and be flooded with an overwhelming sense of wonder and gratitude.

My reverie was interrupted by a big event. It was visitors' time. Visitors' time consisted of two two-hour periods a week, one on Wednesday and one on Saturday. After long intervals between the two days, someone from the outside looked marvelous. If you weren't fortunate enough to have a visitor, then you hung on every word said at the adjoining bedside.

This day, my visitors were late. I watched Janet talking animatedly with a tall gentleman in a dog collar (the rather facetious description we college students had for a clergyman's white clerical garb). He looked at me and smiled. He had the kindest eyes I'd ever seen. I was sure he knew Jesus. He turned back to Janet, and I guessed they were talking about me. I heard my name.

Suddenly he rose and came over to my bed. Without any preamble whatsoever he announced, "Hello, I'm Robert Neil, a friend of Janet's. She's told me you have accepted Christ today."

"Yes," I replied, stunned. He began to say something more, but my eyes had left him, my attention caught by a bright coat and a rowdy clatter of student feet as my three best friends cantered down the slippery floor of the ward. Skidding to a stop at the side of my bed, they looked in amazement at the Reverend Robert. Then they gazed at me in consternation and inquired, in a most concerned manner, if I were all right. The fact of a clergyman at *my* bedside could only mean one thing, as far as they were concerned—the time had come for the last rites.

Robert Neil smiled cheerfully at them and returned to Janet's bedside. My friends were, obviously, highly relieved and began to giggle hysterically. "Jill—how funny! What was he saying to you?" Sharon, my roommate at the time, asked.

I flushed. "He's nice," I said quietly. My friends exchanged looks and then began to bandy around tidbits of college gossip. I looked at them intently and tried to concentrate on what they were saying. Why couldn't I enjoy the juicy news that spilled from their lips? They were my very special friends. My best friends. They meant everything to me. Suddenly, I knew why I couldn't concentrate on their news. I was subconsciously wondering about their reaction when they would find out about my new experience. Actually, I wasn't wondering about their reaction—I was wondering about my reaction to their reaction, for I knew exactly what their attitude would be. It would be what *my* attitude would have been had one of them flipped her lid and gone all religious.

The little blue booklet lay on my bedside table. There hadn't been time to cover it up. The inevitable happened. A silence fell as all three girls fixed their eyes upon the illuminated title, "Becoming a Christian." Nothing was said. I began to talk. Loudly and excitedly, I recounted my time in the hospital and my infatuation with the young interns. I tried to be amusing and light, just the same as I had always been. I wanted them to know I hadn't changed, so I sought to be flippant and funny. But they didn't respond and soon said their good-byes, going on their way down the ward as loudly as they had come.

I lay still, very still. They were gone. Not just from the ward and my bedside—they were gone from me. I knew it and I grieved, because from somewhere deep within, the strong, sure knowledge flooded upward that the friendship of Jesus was going to make a difference in all my relationships. It had to. Why it had to, I knew not, but change there would be. Change I didn't dare to think about.

Shutting my eyes, I tried to blot out the picture of my friends' curious, sidelong looks at my little blue booklet. There was a slight supercilious sneering, as if to say: *Jill? No. Not Jill! Anyone else but her.* I tried not to think of what their conversation would be once they were around the corner of the ward and out of sight.

When I opened my eyes again, visiting time was over, and Janet and I were alone. I turned my back on her and pretended to be tired. I needed time to think. Later, she told me that she had prayed for me—hard—just when I'd needed it. My rather wild companions and their reactions had not gone unnoticed.

"Lord, if she's ever going to make it, help me to prepare her for what's back there at college," she had said to God.

She didn't have much time left—just a few short days before I would be well enough to return to my studies—but it was time that she used to the fullest. Robert Neil bought me a Bible, like Janet's. Into the handbag went Janet's hand, again and again, producing other little booklets like the first one, and they helped me begin to understand what had happened to me.

I peppered her with questions, knowing that once I was discharged I wouldn't be able to have such a mine of useful information in the next bed. In fact, I might have a land mine named Sharon instead. So I ventured to ask Janet what I should do about my friends.

"Just be careful how you share your new faith with them," she cautioned. I had hoped she would advise me how to hide the evidence, but here she was telling me to show it all. "You know, under all that brave exterior, they are probably as empty and searching as you have been," she mused.

I muttered, "I suppose I had better find out," but I wondered despairingly to myself how ever could I do that. "Janet, I'll lose them," I said desperately.

"What sort of friends are they, if they ditch you just because you've found a faith that helps you and makes you happy?" she asked.

"I don't know what sort of friends they are," I replied defensively. "All I know is, I like them and they mean a lot to me, and I don't want to lose them."

"Well, if you do," she replied cheerfully, "God will give you other friends."

"But I don't *want* other friends," I argued petulantly, "I want them."

How could I make Janet understand how very important my friends were to me? To make a friend had always been a must with me. Not a maybe, but a must. As a teenager I had jealously won or bought my friends in various ways. I *had* to have someone to trust and love and talk to for hours and hours on the phone. Someone to share my joys and fears. One who wouldn't steal my boyfriend, or betray my confidence, or sit next to someone else at the movies.

Now, for the very first time in my life, I realized that if I went on in this "Christian life" thing, I would be deliberately giving friendships away—or, at the very least, putting them in jeopardy.

Janet laughed and told me not to worry so much. "Worry empties today of its strength, so you're finished by the time tomorrow's problems come," she said. "Read these booklets. They'll give you some of your answers."

So I did. Settling down, I began to absorb the facts about conversion. I read Psalm 23 about the Good Shepherd and Psalm 19 about God declaring Himself in His marvelous Word. I read that the law of the Lord was perfect, converting the soul, and I knew that that was what had happened to me. I'd been converted—turned right around till I was facing in a totally new direction.

"Any old fish can swim with the stream," Janet commented, "but it takes a live one to swim against it."

"But how shall I do that?" I wailed. "How shall I know what to do . . . and how will I ever get enough strength to do it?"

"The Holy Spirit will give you the strength."

I gazed at her with wide eyes. The Holy Spirit? Whatever did she mean? Now, at this point, if Janet had told me the moon was made of cheese, I would have gladly believed her. I was happy to believe her now, but I hadn't the foggiest notion what she was talking about. "What on earth is the Holy Spirit?" I asked. Somewhere the term rang a familiar bell.

Then I remembered. Standing in the demure rows of students at Homerton College, I had listened respectfully to our college principal intoning old English prayers at our daily assembly. That's where I had heard about it. But it wasn't the Holy Spirit—though it sounded something like it. Thinking hard, I visualized the wizened face of our principal—cracked with knowledgeable age and nursing laser beam eyes, which swept over the lines of promising youth awaiting her directions.

"I believe in the Holy Ghost," she would say. That was it. The Holy Ghost thing. It was a beautifully couched prayer, but had had little effect on my inquiring mind, since someone had told me she thought the lady intoning it didn't even believe in God.

Somehow, not to believe in God at all wasn't "quite on," as we say in the Home Country. Not to believe in a Holy Ghost, however, was understandably permissible. I mean, ghosts and ghouls and four-legged beasties were for the birds. I had given the term "Holy Ghost" fleeting analysis. Fertile pictures of a halo-bedecked wispy spook haunting old English graveyards wafted across my mind. No, I could forgive our principal for not believing in one of those.

But here was Janet telling me about the Holy Spirit—who was obviously related to the Holy Ghost. *He was going to stay with me forever,* she said firmly.

Seeing my alarm, she laughed. I was so glad to see it was all right to laugh in the still point. It didn't seem to break the spell. Somewhere I had got hold of the idea that laughter was to be hung up, with coat and umbrella, at the church door.

"Don't worry about it, Jill," she said. "Just think of it this way: The Holy Spirit is all of God, and all of God is now in all of you. That's all you need to know. You've got all you're getting, so just know it, believe it, and enjoy it . . . all!"

I climbed into that hospital bed for the last time and read Psalm 19 again. Tomorrow I would leave the safety of the hospital and return to college. I was somehow at peace. *All of God in all of me,* I thought. That should do it.

Then I took a last look around. How could it be that those patients still lay like white-trussed turkeys, unaware of my unspeakable joy and wholeness of personality? How could it be that even Praying Mantis, furiously writing reports, looked so very good to me? And Maureen—poor sour, bitter Maureen. Suddenly, with deep certainty I knew the reason for her impatient and unloving behavior. She needed to be forgiven much so that she could love much, that was all.

My still point continued. I had simply moved right along into the middle of it and, settling down, found myself home at last. I thought of Grace, and I decided when I got back to college I would knock softly on her door and step into her room to tell her what was in my heart. I would drop to my knees, with my face also toward the Rising Son. Then she would know the daystar had arisen in my life as well.

Janet was saying something. In the darkness of the ward, I could see her dancing eyes and her beautiful mop of gleaming dark curls, lying starkly against the white pillow. I had never seen anyone so beautiful. How could I ever repay her? How could she know that, all my life, I'd been trying to be like someone else, and—naturally and humanly speaking—at that moment, if I had been true to form, I should be wanting to be like her. Yet, for the very first time in my life, I was content to be me. Why, if I tried to be anyone else at this moment, I would miss the excruciating pleasure of knowing that God filled my soul with His glad Presence. No, I didn't desire to be anyone else but me, and *that* was the miracle. It was just as if I'd held my breath all my life and then I'd let it out—for I now knew it was all right to stop performing and rest in the fact that *He loved me as I was.* Not the me that tried to be like my sisters—serene Grace, or neat Elizabeth, or even the women of my own fertile imagination—but the me who belonged to God.

I knew then it was going to be all right to go home to college. Janet would not be there, but He was already there in the person of His Holy Spirit. And not only that, I had in my possession minute instructions from One who was greater than Janet, and wiser than Grace, and more clever than Elizabeth—the Writer of Psalm 19 Himself. The Law of the Lord would be sufficient, because . . .

> *The Eternal's law is a sound law,*
> *reviving life;*
> *the Eternal's is a trusty witness,*
> *that instructs the open-minded;*
> *the Eternal's orders are just,*
> *a joy to the heart;*
> *the Eternal's command is clear,*
> *a light to the mind;*
> *the Eternal's faith is a clean faith,*
> *it will last for ever;*
> *the Eternal's rulings are upright,*
> *and altogether just—*
> *more to be prized than gold,*
> *than plenty of rare gold,*
> *sweeter than honey itself,*
> *than honey from the comb.*
> *Yes, and by them thy servant takes warning;*
> *in following them there is rich profit.*
> *Psalm 19:7–11*

To Be a Friend: Application and Journal

....

1. How important is it to you that you have friends? Are you satisfied with the number of friends you have and the depth of your relationship with them?

2. How secure are you in the following areas:
   Christ's friendship   _____
   the unconditional love
         of at least one friend   _____
   freedom to be real
         rather than seek
         conformity to others   _____
   freedom to love others
         who can't "give back" to you   _____
   freedom to release friendships that
         may be harmful spiritually
         or in other ways   _____

3. Do you remember the person who led you to the Lord? Write a brief thank-you note to God for what you remember about that person.

4. Who has God brought into your life who needs to know Christ as Savior? (Don't forget family members, coworkers, or neighborhood children.) What would they be likely to say about you as a Christian based on your love (John 13:35)?

. . . .

For Action:
Think of one person with whom you don't normally seek out interaction—
an unbeliever or someone you consider "unlovely."
Commit to pray daily for that person.

. . . .

Chapter Four

Elspeth

*B*ack at college, aware my soul had been turned around, I began to pick up my fractured plans and the slack of classes missed. Conscious of an inner pull in a new direction, I found my thought patterns kaleidoscoping into new colors, fresh caution tempering my usual quick reactions, and the strangest thing of all—a deep concern for friends with problems made a home in, not just an occasional visit to, my heart.

These new attitudes led me to discover something else: I wanted to serve me! The Law of the Lord had indeed converted my soul. But just how did one start to serve others? It was a sad state of affairs, as I racked my brain, wondering how to serve other people, until I realized that eighteen years of my life had been spent expecting everyone else to serve me. That was going to take a lot of *unlearning.* I couldn't remember any courses or books offered on the subject of servanthood. There had undoubtedly been many marvelous models around, starting with my own sweet, serving mother; but other heroes, in school history books or movies, had been exotic characters who served only their country, their own ideas, or their girlfriends. Albert Schweitzer was the only one I could think of who truly appeared to have served God. *Was that how?* I wondered. *Did serving God mean dashing around some tropical jungle with a butterfly net, trying to convert natives, or playing an organ hymn in some steamy place?* No. Somehow all that didn't seem to fit.

What was I expected to do with all of this spiritual energy striving to release itself? Totally ignorant of God's intentions toward me, I turned to the Eternal One, who told me He would instruct the open-minded.

"Fling open the shuttered windows of your thoughts toward heaven and let Me tell you what to do," He said. So, with eyes screwed up like wrinkled sand and body shaped into a ball of tense expectancy, I strained to hear the voice that never came. It never came because it had already come. The law—the Law of the Eternal—and not some mystic voice, was to instruct my open mind. *But how?* I asked myself. Just where did I begin to read the Bible?

At the beginning? That seemed to be a good notion. A beginner should start at the beginning, and this beginner did.

"In the beginning God," it said. Oh yes, I replied. Yes, please—yes now! For, like the earth, I too need Your Spirit to move upon the face of my original chaos. I read His ordered orders and watched the plants and vegetation bloom to His command. Quite right, I thought. God said—and it was so. God said—and it was so; God said and it was so. The rhythm of obedience beat out the praise of things alive, who knew that without the thoughtfulness of the Original Thought, their being would never have been at all.

But oh, the woman! Susceptible to subtle serpent, I watched her listening to the voice of vice. "Don't serve God—make Him serve *you.* Usurp the orders of Eternal Law and decide your own doings," he said.

And so she did—and so had I. For eighteen years my doings and decidings had been determined by desire. Now at last my "doings" and "decidings" must be determined by God's demands. I discovered "demands" meant "commands," and, like Eve, having been chased into glad capture and confession, I was ready to obey.

Leafing through the pages of the Bible, I discovered a prayer in the Psalms I could not have said better myself. "Open thou mine eyes, that I may behold wondrous things out of thy law," it said (Psalm

119:18). Someone else must have had the same problem I did. *Who was this man praying for insight?* I wondered. Was it permissible to pray that the Eternal would make His mind known to little "mud men" like us? It seemed so, for however simple our construction, the mind of man—the forgiven mind, that is—had been equipped to catch the waves of words from heaven. *The forgiven one, yes, but does that only mean the clever one?* I wondered. Did the Bible promise this wisdom only to the wise? No, it was actually promised to the simple, I noted— to the forgiven simple! Wow. Tossing that thought through the windows of my reasonings, God exploded my fear that I might be too stupid to comprehend, for to hear and understand His voice had suddenly become more important to me than anything else on earth. I remembered Janet saying that the Holy Spirit would be with me as my Teacher, and I wondered what sort of Instructor He would turn out to be. Would Eternal Intelligence really put up with such simplicity as mine?

I had a fleeting vision of my grade school days. I remembered a strangely shaped math teacher. She reminded me of an angry frog looking for a poor fly like me. She would consistently order me to the front of the class and stand me in front of the blackboard with a piece of new chalk in my hand. Then she ceremoniously piled the awful and mysterious symbols of math on top of each other, making them look like some primitive dread funeral pyre. "Work it out, Jill," she croaked triumphantly. With a mind anesthetized by fear into "math amnesia," I shuffled from one shoe to the other, sometimes having to stay there until the class was over. Then the chalk was snatched away and the "frog" chortled in a throttled voice, "You're stupid!" I believed her, of course, but the thing that hurt most was a sense that she was secretly glad I was so simple. I knew she didn't like me.

Being concerned with the welfare of the poor, it fell to her lot to collect the "charity penny" from each girl in her class. This "penny" was not required but supposedly was a voluntary affair. One day I forgot. The frog never did. Stopping me in the wooded and austere hallway, she demanded to know the "cruel motivation" that led to the withholding of my abundant wealth from the poor. In vain I insisted I had forgotten. How on earth my charity penny could possibly alleviate such a catalogue of dire distress as she was busy enumerating was completely beyond me, but that was the day my math ordeal began.

Jesus, however, was inviting me to learn of Him. He was to be my Teacher—and I discovered that to be a pupil of Jesus was to come to know a very gentle and humble-minded Instructor who was never impatient with slow learners. He would not stand me in front of His Word for hours on end only to pronounce at the termination of my misery, "You're stupid." No, no—even though He was thoroughly acquainted with the extent of my simplicity, He had committed Himself to making me spiritually wise. I couldn't wait to begin my lessons. But unfortunately there was a problem. Just where could I go to read my Bible? Surrounded as I was by girls, girls, and more girls—and with them noise, noise, and more noise—where on campus could I find a place to be alone with God?

"What's wrong with your own bedroom?" a small inner voice suggested. I ignored it. Sharon, my roommate, would be there, and I could just imagine her face as she watched me learn my "spiritual math." I thought about Joan. Joan was a big, happy corridor representative who believed in God and read her Bible every day. Maybe she would be kind enough to allow me the use of her bedside. When I asked her, she smiled a wide happy smile and said, "Of course—come on in any time." She was great. She didn't even ask me why I didn't want to pray in my own room, but instead set about suggesting what I should study and how I could hunt for God's promises, commands, and warnings in the verses of Scripture. She showed me how to mark them in different colors so I could remember them. She explained how to pray about the discoveries I would make, and so my happy search began. I found it was all true . . .

> The Eternal's law was indeed—
> Sweeter than honey
> Finer than gold.

I didn't know that the time was coming to test the sterling worth of some of those promises I was finding in my spiritual treasury.

The morning started just like all the rest—tumbling out of bed, Sharon and I laughed and joked our way through morning preparations for the busy day ahead. Tucking my Bible away between the books for my first class, I slipped out of our room and along the corridor to Joan's. Tapping insistently upon the closed door, I couldn't imagine why she wasn't answering. Glancing down at the floorboards, I saw the light was on, so I knew she was "at home." A strange foreboding "boded" along the corridor and sat on my heart. After what seemed an interminably long time, the door was unlocked and Joan's sweet, sympathetic—but very determined—face placed itself against the crack.

"Jill—it's time you nailed your colors to the mast," she said quietly through the aperture. "Sharon has to be told sometime, so go back to your own room and talk to God there!" So saying, she snapped the door shut and there I was, left standing in the long, empty corridor wondering how on earth she could do that to me.

I remembered Grace, and my mind went back to the moment I had stood in her room and watched her pray. I had a silly urge to run upstairs and beg her to come and "do it again" in front of Sharon this time, but I knew immediately that it would never do, for now it was my turn, and there was no one in the whole wide world who could do it for me.

Trundling back to our room, I was relieved to discover Sharon had gone to breakfast. Maybe if I rushed I could get it over before she returned. I began to scramble through my devotions. Needless to say, I couldn't concentrate at all. Futilely searching for some relevant help, I glanced at the clock and decided it was time to pray.

Somehow my knees found their lowly destination. There I stayed tensely listening, not for the Eternal's instructions, but for the footsteps of my departing friendship. Thinking of Sharon eating her toast and marmalade, oblivious to the trauma of the incident that lay ahead, absorbed my whole being. Why, oh why, was this one of the hardest things I had ever done?

I thought of my childhood years when my friends and I had played the game of "truth, dare, force, or promise." If you chose "truth," you were bound to answer honestly any question asked. A "dare" could be attempted or refused. "Force" meant a chase through the garden and a physical free-for-all as you wrestled out of the imaginative challenges thought up for you. But a "promise" was something else. I was brought up in a culture that had taught me "An Englishman's word is his bond." A promise was a promise, implying implicit obedience.

All my friends had been pretty rowdy and wild, and yet it was always I who would go for the promise. I thought of the time I walked the rafters of a bombed-out house, literally taking my life in my hands. I had stopped strangers in the street and asked them what they had had for breakfast, jumped from a ridiculously high wall onto railroad tracks when I could see a train approaching, and even sneaked up the back stairs of a total stranger's house, right up to the attic and down again—all for the sake of my word. I was only a mad twelve years old when I did all that—so what was the matter with me now? To kneel and pray in front of my best friend because of His Word and His promise was by far the most scary thing I had ever done.

Still I knelt there. I wondered if my face looked anything like Grace's had looked, or if she'd had to practice for hours on end in order to glow like that. Jumping up I peered into the mirror to see if I was shining, only to be met by two wide, frightened eyes and a trembling mouth. Down I went again. My knees were killing me. Not being used to such long pious exercise, I wondered if I could pray kneeling on a cushion or if that wasn't allowed. *I must remember to ask Janet,* I thought.

Suddenly I heard Sharon's footsteps. I still had time to get up, but I didn't. The door crashed open, and she saw me kneeling there, my body language implying, "This is how it is, Sharon. I'm down on my knees with my face to the Rising Son" (except it felt like all the world to me as if the sun had just sunk). With a burden in my heart, I knew I was saying good-bye.

I was right. Too right. It wasn't even *au revoir*—Sharon never spoke a word to me again, and we finished out the year in that confined space in the chilly isolation of silence. Each day I tried a new tactic, making her bed or supplying some tasty supper morsel, just about everything I could think of that would force her to say at least a "thank-you," but it was never said.

She reported my "odd" behavior to our gang, and they stopped asking me to the jazz band events we used to go to before I had gone to the hospital. No more party invitations came my way. It hurt being left out. How could it be that friendship with God should have such drastic repercussions upon my earthly relationships? Why were my friends so disgusted with my newfound faith? Was it perhaps that they couldn't believe it was real and thought me hypocritical? I didn't know, and as they wouldn't let me ask them, I looked around for other friends.

I didn't have to look far. They were there all the time. Joan, Fiona, Viviane, and Ann. Juliet and Margaret and Elizabeth. Betty and Angela, Pauline and Doreen. And Elspeth. It was Elspeth who took my hand and began to introduce me to this huge "family" I'd never met before and yet who seemed strangely and endearingly familiar to me. It was that same "family likeness" I recognized in Grace and Janet that linked us all together, proving us "blood sisters" not of human line, but of the Christ whose life was given for us and under whose wings we had come to trust. God's forever family, I was soon to discover, treated me like family too.

"Why don't you start looking a man straight in the eye instead of fluttering your eyelashes at him like that?" asked Grace. I practiced in the mirror. It was hard at first but produced good solid brother friendships among my new peers. I took her no-flirting admonition a further step and quit wearing makeup.

"Why have you taken off all your makeup?" inquired another, as we had a sisterly talk one day.

"Because," I answered earnestly, "I was wearing it to attract boys."

"Well," she replied, "you won't need to worry anymore!"

Yes, it was "family treatment," and I loved it. Fancy being free to receive criticism without it leveling, or worse still, burying me. Now I had someone to give it and somewhere to go with it. I could climb into my still point and talk to God about it, and I did. "About the 'eye thing,' Lord," I asked, "what have You got to say about that?" He told me that Job was one of His friends who had had an eye problem too. Every time a pretty maid walked by, his eyes would walk right along with her. So he made a promise not to look upon a maid like that. I decided I would take a leaf out of his book. That was a new experience for me—and for the men in my life.

"What about the makeup thing?" I asked Him next.

"Consider the lilies," He answered, and I did—and found them absolutely gorgeous. They were so natural, and that helped me to see He was saying that I needed to be natural too. "When you've found out your character," it seemed He was telling me, "dress to match. Just be the lily I made you to be, for even Solomon in all his glory was not arrayed like one of these."

"But, Lord," I countered rather peevishly, "nobody has to *look* at me; after all, from now on my life is going to be spent in prayer and Bible study, so who's going to care?"

"If that's the plan—I have to look at you," I thought I heard Him say. Well! That was a new thought. Up to this critical point in my life, I had dressed exclusively for my friends, not just the boyfriends, but the girlfriends too. In becoming a believer, I had simply transferred my anxiety about pleasing my old friends to anxiety about pleasing my new ones. Seeking to conform to a few dowdy and drab disciples, I had lowered my hems and buttoned up to my neck. Now here was the Lord telling me to look a little further and notice not a few of His family who were subtly and smartly clad. They were dressing for Him.

I decided to try to be a lily—not a weed. My clothes could show a freedom to be my own person, preaching a sermon loud and clear that would say, "God made me—unique and different from all other flowers of the field. I will dress to enhance the physical best He has graced me with."

My new girlfriends introduced me to their boyfriends, and their boyfriends introduced me to their girlfriends, and they all introduced me to their programs of study and fellowship. "What's fellowship?" I whispered to Grace.

"Two fellows in a ship," she quipped back. "Sharing the ups and downs together and talking about the challenges of the Christian life."

"Do Christians do anything else," I ventured to ask, "or is it all religious? Do they play games, and go to movies, or read magazines?"

She laughed, "Of course they do."

"Do they go to dances?" I persisted—"because this boy Peter has asked me to go to a May Ball with him."

Grace spontaneously responded with a hug and a kiss and a glad, "Great, Jill, I'll help you get ready."

I was very relieved, as I'd been so afraid of meeting negativism. I had expected to be told, "Don't do this and you can't be that and don't dare go there." So far I had not met with this attitude at all. In the hospital I had confided to Janet that I feared to commit my life to Christ lest He should make me give things up. She had replied that there were two things He would certainly insist I give up, and they were sin and selfishness. Now that had to be a positive. The girls I met, and the boys for that matter, had majored in the "thou shalts" rather than the "thou shalt nots." I found that if my lifestyle was indeed changing, and I perceived that it was, this was not because I had been told not to be involved in certain things, but it was simply a matter of choosing to spend my time in other pursuits.

A May Ball was the social event of the calendar year. It was a splendid affair beginning with parties in the paneled rooms within the cobbled courtyards of the men's colleges. "Age and wisdom" hung heavy in the air, while youth climbed through the fusty gloom and shouted them away. That balmy night, wisdom sulked behind bookshelves, making room for youth's nonsense. Bands on the lawn. "Tut, tut," said wisdom, but then, nobody was listening—the dance was on.

Peter was sweet. I didn't know him well at all. We sat apart and tried to find some common interest to span our awkwardness. He liked tennis; I sighed—that was good. We spent the hour swapping tennis talk, and I told him I had won a trophy when I was just fourteen years of age. He seemed impressed, and I started wondering what my Christianity would mean to my tennis game. Could a Christian compete, or would my killer instinct now be tempered with grace? I decided that would have to remain a mystery until we played our next college match.

It was time to dance. Inside the walls we shuffled against the crowded bodies, preening and pivoting, proud to be there, to be seen, to be our "best," for after all, we had made it to the ball. I tried to stop looking at the clock. Seeing the festivities had just begun, I couldn't understand why I felt a certain strange impatience.

We walked away from the crowded room and wandered on the trim and tidy lawns. How unbelievably beautiful everything looked. The clipped bushes and manicured greens. The stone gray castle shapes carved against the deep sky. The quiet, sultry River Cam caressing with sweet lapping lips the riverbanks, our world. The winsome weeping willows teased the water with their fingertips and shushed away our cares. And the punts. The funny, flat pontoons, peculiar to our environment, pushed down the stream by the Cambridge Clan—those crazy, clever students who nested here awhile outside the "real" world. They were fun to watch. The idea was to propel the boat with a long pole pushing against the river bed. To push you stood upon a little platform at the back of the punt. The obvious and inevitable laugh was to find oneself hanging on the end of the punt pole outside the boat. Tonight, however, no one was dressed to swim. A far too romantic stage had been set.

Peter was saying something. His hands were clenched and he was perspiring. He didn't look at me but kept muttering about something he *must* say to me. If I had known him a little longer I would have been sure he was going to propose. "What on earth is it?" I asked him curiously.

"Jill, I know you probably won't understand this," he began, "but something happened a few weeks ago that was terribly important to me." He paused, and suddenly an alarm went off inside my heart. I woke up to the sense of destiny I had begun to recognize lately. It was as if I were walking through a maze with Someone watching from above who had the whole puzzle figured out and who had planted people around the corners who would bump into me. Peter was about to bump into me. I knew it, before he ever said a word. He was surely in touch with the maze maker and was about to tell me just that. How "amazed" was he going to be when I matched his news with "Me too, Peter."

At last it was out. He knew Christ. We laughed and shared our experiences and talked both at once and interrupted lovers along the quiet river with our excited chatter.

"Let's get a punt, Jill," Peter suggested. "We can offer to take these loving couples out, and once we've let them cuddle for a minute, you can tell them about Christ while I punt!" We did it. It was a wild idea, but the loving pairs accepted our invitation with only a slightly suspicious stare.

Peter pushed us off, nearly getting left behind in his excitement. "You pray, I'll punt," he whispered at me. The couples kissed and cuddled away until the allotted time, when out of sight and sound of all distractions, we "let them have it." Oh dear, poor things. What a shock! But what adventure for us. Did ever a May Ball afford so many great opportunities before? And then to have one girl accept the Lord! Oh joy. The morning came, and we punted down the waking water for the last time to have breakfast at the Hansel-and-Gretel-like village of Gressingham. We were pretty wet and bedraggled but, oh, how happy. The scrambled eggs and fatty bacon, hot buttered toast and English tea disappeared down our hungry throats as we talked at each other both at once about our grand endeavor.

At nine o'clock back at college, we had to walk down the hall and sign in at the head table in front of all the poor unfortunate students who hadn't had a date. I watched the girls in front of me preening their feathers for the status walk that would say to all their college mates, who sought to eat their food pretending not to care, "We made it, we got asked, and we've had a lovely time." I couldn't wait to take my triumphal march, not to show off, however, but to find Grace and tell her about the marvelous way God had arranged it all. I was simply bursting to tell the news about that precious new friend who had come to Christ sitting in her boyfriend's lap in a punt in the middle of the River Cam. The girl in front of me was talking about the band. *What band?* I thought.

As soon as possible I visited Janet in the hospital. How much I had to tell her. I could hardly wait to report our "grand success" and receive her accolades. The visit was duly made. The report was given, but the appreciation was not forthcoming. "Stop bragging about it," she snapped. "If God has used you, then be grateful, but remember He only uses the stupid so people will know it was His power that did it all." I felt humiliated. But she was certainly right. Suddenly I realized I had been being pretty obnoxious since the dance. I had too soon ceased to be thrilled about Wendy coming to the Lord and started being proud of myself for leading her there.

"Pride is a rotten thing," Janet was saying. "God hates it."

The time was well spent with her that day. She talked long and straight to me, telling how she believed God wanted to use me to help others find Christ just as she had helped me find Him. Looking into her eyes, I knew she wasn't saying "you can"; she was saying "you must." "But, Jill," she added very seriously, "you are going to need someone to keep you humble. I'm going to pray that there will be someone back at Homerton who will be a real friend." The way she said "real friend" made me think of a "real enemy," but she was already leafing through the Law of the Lord—"by which His servants are warned," to find me the little verse that said, "Faithful are the wounds of a friend." I kissed her, bound up my many wounds of the afternoon with the bandage of true friendship, and took my leave.

Returning to college, I met the answer to her prayers. Elspeth. Having already been introduced to her among the group of Christian believers, I began to get to know her a little better. She apparently decided to attach herself to me like a friendly barnacle on a tossing boat—and to hang on. *Bounce.* That's the word that springs to mind about Elspeth. Bounce and twinkle and laughter, too. Lots of it. Loud, raucous, and yet humorously musical. Her mirth met a person early, hurrying ahead of her to announce her happy presence. Naturally golden curls beat time along with the music of her personality. She was such a steady joy to be with, and soon I was humbly grateful to be counted as her friend. She it was who mothered my mistakes, turning them into growing children of experience, insisting I learn how to fail successfully. She refused to allow the fervor of mastering new skills in the Christian life—such as basic prayer habits and Bible study—to turn me into a fanatic. Laughing her way into my intensity, she mellowed my exuberance, as God began to use me in girls' lives. When I started to think myself too important, somehow laughter—Elspeth's laughter—was born along with each project, humbling it into perspective. How could the Christian life be so sweetly funny, I marveled? Elspeth made it so for me.

Audrey was our first combined challenge. After I spent many days building bridges of friendship and many more hours in prayer for her with Elspeth, Audrey knelt beside my bed and prayed the prayer that Janet had said for me. Keeping one eye open to check on the effect of our intercession, I watched eternity crash into time in the person of Christ, and Christmas came at least two calendar months before it was due. Dragging her along to Elspeth's room, we were met with waterfalls of mirth and sweet expressions of hope for Audrey's new life.

Next the three of us met to pray for Penny. She was another kettle of fish. She reminded me very much of myself. We parried and thrust like fencers through many a debate about the existence of God and the deity of Christ. One day I met her on the curling staircase guarding the long, precise corridors of our dorm. Leaning against the banister, she raised a bottle of wine to her lips as I passed her and facetiously inquired if I would take her to church on Sunday if she were sober by then. She wore her short dark hair like a sleek cap, ragged around her puckish face. Her black-brown eyes challenged us to chase her into heaven, and chase her we did. Day by day, Elspeth and I asked God, please, to bring her home. Using the bridge of friendship, we laughed and played together for many, many days. We biked to town and giggled at the little dress shops stocked with slightly outdated women's clothes. We watched old people attending makeup clinics in the marketplace in town. "'Decorated age' is sort of sad," I said to Penny.

"They're papering over the cracks, aren't they?" she rejoined.

"Old people aren't the only ones who do *that!*" I said. She shot me a look and fell quiet. That night, I found her leaning on my doorpost just looking at me, taking a break from her studies, with a sort of fierce intensity. Recognizing the feel of that hungry look, I asked her into my room and soon saw her yield to Christ.

Elspeth, with wisdom beyond her years, saw how very special Penny had become to me. "Mother hen," she teasingly chided. "Give her room to grow. You're smothering her. A parent's job is to bring a child to independence, and you're tying Penny to your spiritual apron strings." It was true. Every time Penny sought to branch out on her own, I was there to "boss" her into submission again. For the first time in my life the roles were reversed and I was the dominating one. The links were strong, for a deep spiritual bond had been forged between us. She even lovingly called me "Mom." I understood her, and what was more, God had given us a sweet, caring concern for each other. But love lets go or love can corrupt, and once again it was Elspeth who helped me set Penny free to breathe and become the new person she had been born again to be, and not simply a carbon copy of her spiritual mom. She managed to tease us away from an intense relationship that could have destroyed the very love we sought to keep.

The summer was coming, and Elspeth and I signed up together for a beach mission. Forty students were to pile into a beach house and for the Kingdom's sake, work their way into youngsters' hearts and souls.

Back home, I told my parents of my desire to join the team, and they agreed to let me go. My father gave me a surprise present of a huge "scooter," quite the new thing in England at the time, deciding I could be an advertisement for his new merchandise—an idea with which I was more than happy to comply. I could ride it all the way down England to Frinton on Sea and to the beach mission. But first I had to learn to drive the thing. After supper the night of the presentation of my gift, my dad set me off to practice, giving me all relevant instructions except the most important one—how to stop. Around and around the block I went until at last the machine ran out of gas and I fell off against our garage doorpost.

It was exciting buying all the equipment for my new machine. The waterproofs and Wellingtons and various Mackintosh cover-ups—for everyone knows there are only two seasons in England: winter, and the second week of August. I dreamed away the days of preparation, imagining myself as some brave modern Joan of Arc serving God—not on a white horse, but on a red motor scooter.

I was so excited that I was going to learn how to be a servant. The leaders would teach our small but dedicated community how to serve God, each other, and the families that gathered year by year for their annual vacations. Once we arrived I discovered that all our combined talents were needed. Those of us who could draw made visual aids and publicity posters. Those who could sing or play a portable instrument composed songs of Scripture with rhythms that beat with the throb of God's love. Those who could talk prepared the Bible lessons; they broke truth into small enough pieces for the littlest child to digest. The sand pulpit had to be dug each day and little salt-sticky hands recruited to decorate, with shells and beach flowers, words of Him who long ago wrote words with His finger in another pile of sand. Someone had to invite people to the daily services. *We* had to tell them. This was it.

To walk up to total strangers, crossing that forbidden British distance of privacy and reserve, and "push our wares" upon them was not easy. "What are you selling?" sniped a cheeky kid.

"It's free," I answered.

"Can't be worth much then," shot back the careless sally.

Red-tinged necks of embarrassment, hot palms clutching handouts, faltering words of eager faith, hot sand-slowing pounding steps along the crowded beach, and faces faintly supercilious—mostly annoyed with our interruptions—all were part and parcel of our day's work. Back home vegetables had to be peeled. Chopping them in half to quicken the chore, I was rebukingly reminded it was God's money I was wasting. Oh how much I learned! But one thing above all others: it was *much, much* better to give than to receive. Serving was fun—hard, sometimes bittersweet, but always exhilarating and accompanied with an enabling energy that defied description. I had not yet learned the verse that promised "Faithful is he that calleth you, who also will do it," but the experience of it was mine, and I knew I would never be the same again.

"When I get home after college," I confided to Elspeth, "I want to do this there."

"In Liverpool?" she asked incredulously.

"Yes, in Liverpool," I answered determinedly. "Teenagers must be the same in any place. All we have to do is to put these same principles we are learning here into action there. Go where the kids are and don't expect them to come to us, and present them with a bright enthusiastic 'doing' involvement with Christ. It has to work." Elspeth grinned acceptance and challenged me to a "peel a potato" race in the kitchen.

I couldn't believe Christians could have so much fun together. On our one day off a week we'd pile into the few vehicles we had among us and roar around the coast line, investigating God's wasteland of sea grass and His flats laced and braceleted with silver bands of water. Elspeth and two lads drove their sports car too far out and got caught by the tide. It was Elspeth who insisted on staying as long as possible with the sinking ship, teasing and chiding the guys as we pulled the submerged vehicle out by sheer body power.

Sweet Elspeth, what a legacy of joy and friendship you left me! Thank you.

Back at college she continued to tone down fervor and cut me down to size, seeking to stop me from becoming a pious bore. One day walking into my room with a new soft light in her eyes and a golden kitten chuckle on her breath, she murmured, "He's nice—oh, Jill—so sweet," and she was gone. Having fallen in love with her man, she was carried off to an island in the sun in the English Channel—and I saw her no more. Grace married her famous cricketer, Penny began to court a quiet, adoring giant, and that left me. Maybe there would be one for me too, I fantasized. A tall, dark, handsome Christian—somewhere, someplace, who would carry me off to some needy mission field where we would serve God together. But I didn't dare ask the Lord about it. I was scared that if I did, He might say no.

To Be a Friend: Application and Journal

....

1. If you have a friend who holds you accountable, write how that relationship has been profitable. If you do not, how would such a relationship be beneficial? Who are some people in your life who might be willing to be "real friends"?

2. In the space below, make a list of the people who have left you a legacy of friendship.

3. What are some things you have learned from friends?

4. Do you have a tendency to smother friends who are a little way "ahead" of you or to hold onto people you are discipling? (If you are unsure, ask someone who is observant and honest—or assume the answer is yes.) What are some specific, realistic boundaries you can set up to allow your relationship(s) some room to breathe?

. . . .

For Action:
From the people whose names you mentioned in questions 1 and 2, call one person and invite her to do something "just for fun." Try to think of something one of you has never done or wouldn't ordinarily do.

. . . .

Chapter Five

....

Ann

....

Graduation. A piece of paper, a handshake, a swift parental embrace, and the ignorance of the young was mine to conquer. "Begone, foul fiend," I snarled at Ignorance. Metaphorically brandishing in his face my diploma, fresh off the graduation press, I fully expected him to turn tail and run. He didn't. He met my challenge, standing his ground and flaunting his authority within the classroom walls of my first assignment. With the flush of youthful idealism, I searched the runny-nosed, leaky-eyed baby faces for a sign of the fitting hunger for knowledge a first-time student at the tender age of four should carry into school. I searched in vain, however, and experienced instead a certain shaking of my grand resolves. It was not going to be quite as I imagined. To have accumulated facts to teach was one thing, but actually to "do it" was going to be another.

The entire room appeared to be filled with child-shaped mobiles, chinking and clattering against each other as they spun around among themselves, thoroughly bewildered by the strangeness of it all. The tenuous thread of parental desire that had suspended them in this foreign place troubled them greatly.

So many questions had been left, like them, "hanging in the air." Where had Mother gone? When would she come back? *Would* she return at all? Why had this cruel conspiracy been contrived to leave them clutching the paper bags filled with mysteriously wrapped sandwiches? Was the food to last all day, or was it for tomorrow too? Why was that little boy eating his now, and why was he starting to eat the little girl's next to him as well? And where, oh where, was the familiar plastic plate and cup with the funny pink bunny on the outside? Who was the strange lady sticking up above the rest of the little people like a lamppost? And most important of all, what were all the other children doing here?

In some children each stranger's face produced sheer panic, in some hostility—but here and there, with staunch traditional resolve, a small child stood aloof as if to say, "I say, old chap, we know the ship is sinking—but hang it all—some cool heads are needed around this place." Stiff upper lips were, however, few and far between, lower trembling ones being much more in evidence. A few toddlers refused to take their coats off. After all, why take it off when you've decided not to stay?

One little lad, marooned upon a table, fastened his eyes firmly on his sandals. Hadn't the teacher just told him his shoes were getting too small? How long would it be before they disappeared? It was all very confusing as he hadn't even noticed them shrinking before this awful day.

A curled and crisp young lady lowered herself, her lunch box, and her varied teddy bears and dolls onto a little painted chair. It had been very difficult to know which chair to choose. How could you tell if it was yours or not? And was it safe to sit on? She wondered what the trash collector was doing outside the big, wide window. Where did he take all the rubbish? Did he take it to his house? Did he have a mother?

The little girl seemed unbelievably unaware of the child next to her, who was screaming and kicking at a closed door with the handle too high to reach. My attention was caught by two children between whom stretched an elongated doll. One little dear had her fingernails embedded in its eye and ear, while the other shrieked in high-pitched fury as she wrenched the doll's ankle round and round trying to dislocate her opponent's arm. *How childish*, I thought briefly, as I joined the fray. *Why get so wound up over a doll?* Didn't they know about the troubles in Ireland or the starving millions? Why didn't they just grow up and act their age? Realizing in the next instant that that was exactly what they were doing, I passed by on the other side and sought to referee more serious confrontations.

As I billed and cooed about the room like some agitated dove, the chaos intensified. I wondered bitterly whose bright idea it was to start all the newcomers off on the same day. I had a mental picture of the Praying Mantis and the Black Widow sending a sneaky letter to the Board of Education about me, instructing them to place me in the worst of school situations—thus finishing my career before it ever got off the ground. I suddenly noticed a little girl at my side. She was riveted to the spot, clutching her ankle and struggling to lift her foot off the floor. Great blobs of misery coursed down her cheeks and splashed upon her shoes. "What's the matter?" I asked sympathetically. She didn't answer, so I investigated and discovered her footwear glued securely down by a huge glob of freshly spewed out chewing gum.

"It is time to tiptoe to the toilets, children," I yelled brightly over the bedlam. As I opened up the classroom door I distinctly remembered one college instructor warning us that the first visit to this very necessary place could turn out to be a traumatic event. I couldn't imagine at the time what prompted that comment, but I was soon to find out. The little boys refused en masse to "go" while everyone else was watching them, and the little girls regarded the small pink cells with dark suspicion. If they went in there, would they ever come out again?

It was at this point that two of the gang went "over the wall." Off I set in hot pursuit, pounding my way across the playground to the music of the howls of a skinny little fellow who had figured out where to sit, but had omitted to hold on. Followed by not a few little shadows pulling up their pants, I nabbed the first runaway at the gate; he bit the back of my hand. Resisting a most un-Christian urge to bite him back, I carried him indoors with not a little difficulty. To my utter dismay, I was greeted by the ominous form of my headmistress from whose firm fist dangled the second sprinter. How awful. What on earth would she think of her new teacher? Without a word, she barreled ahead of me, like a stately ship in full sail, into the classroom, and the children tumbled around like waves before her bow. Issuing commands in what can only be described as a "bullying love tone," she compelled instant, awed silence.

Sweeping up stray children like some giant grab, she came to rest on the large wooden teacher's desk. Plunking a boy's well-spanked bottom firmly on her ample knees she demanded in a stentorian voice, "Now then, give me a kiss." A kiss! *Never,* I thought. *He'll never kiss her after that.* Hadn't I been told at Cambridge that you never spanked a child in the first place? Incredulously I watched the little chap reach quickly up and wind eager arms around her neck. The kiss was given, and the child snuggled down against her in obvious enjoyment.

"A child who does what it likes doesn't like what it does," she commented briefly. "These children must learn to do what *you* like them to do, Miss Ryder; then they'll feel secure." Throwing her head back, she gave a great, deep guffaw. The children caught her mood, relaxed, and gratefully smiled their way into her solid self-assuredness. Like some happy sergeant she chided the two little soldiers who had gone AWOL and, winking at me, made her grand exit. At the door she paused, turned around, and told me to let her handle the mothers.

"Which mothers?" I asked, bewildered.

"The ones who'll be after you with their umbrellas for clobbering their Harry or Tommy or whoever," she retorted. "Leave them to me. You'll soon learn we are not dealing with delinquent kids but with delinquent parents." She marched back into the room, retrieved a large piece of chalk from the blackboard, and launched herself into the playground toward a fence over which hung some fearsome-looking Liverpool moms.

Drawing a line on the tarmac indicating forbidden territory, she brandished her chalk on high and shouted at the women, "Thus far and no farther! Don't you dare put one toe over that mark, or I'll be after you!"

A little later, as I took my first playground duty, I asked myself just what I had gotten myself into. Was this the teaching profession or vice patrol? On entering the classroom again, I noticed one little boy who had not been out to play but had fallen asleep across his desk. "'Is paw goes to the pub and doesn't get 'ome till late," his friend explained. Who was his "paw" and which "pub"? I wondered.

Out "there," beyond the confines of my duty and my experience, lay the answers and my mission field. I knew it that very first day of orientation, when the children of Liverpool drenched my life— touched my heart strings and set me off to insist on knowing what lay beyond.

Beyond what? Beyond the four-year-old's lunch box, beyond the frightened little one who wouldn't let me touch him, beyond the red welt across a little girl's cheek. Beyond four o'clock in the afternoon when my job should really be over and my rest earned. I had to go beyond. "The little further" that was not required beckoned me because I served Him. Where did all my children live? What hell did some emerge from daily? What sort of teenagers were their big brothers and sisters? I was soon to find out.

The mother of a child in my class confided in me that her teenage son was giving them a great deal of trouble. It was her second marriage, and John resented his new father. Would I speak to him? I set a time and place in a restaurant and met the boy. He had the most honest face I'd ever seen. He listened earnestly while I pleaded with him to let God handle his life. Accompanying me to my church, he agreed to pray with me. Kneeling beside him in the still air of that chapel, I became in my imaginings a female George Mueller, tending the poor little lambs that had gone astray.

As we left, we bumped into the silver-haired, venerable secretary of the fellowship. Babbling out the story of John's misdoings and reformation, I introduced them to each other. The older man smiled in a sort of confused way and shook his hand. We left. Unknown to me, John lifted the man's gold cigarette case and wallet in passing. So much for my convert! Things deteriorated from then on, culminating that night in the most dramatic scene in John's house, as his stepfather called the police to come and arrest him.

Standing there aghast, watching that young man pack his case for prison, I could hardly believe my ears when the officer ordered me into the squad car as well. Midnight found me at the police station sitting in a shattered little heap of discouragement, having had my efforts ridiculed by the somewhat cynical cop. After convincing him I was not John's lover, he set about trying to frighten me to death so that I would stop meddling in dangerous business and above all quit believing my "religion" could possibly change lost causes like John. Feeling completely humiliated, I muttered a stubborn comment about God's ability to change anyone, however bad. Finally I was allowed to go home.

That night searching the Law of the Lord, I read about Jesus in the Garden of Gethsemane and noticed that as He and His disciples went to pray, He "went a little further." His followers slept, but He continued to battle for the souls of mankind. I thought it reasonable for the disciples to take their rest. After all, the sin of the world was a problem far too big for them to handle. Why not let Jesus agonize alone? But as I meditated upon the Son of God asking for their identification, I knew the Eternal was asking for mine as well. That involvement, not in the redemption of mankind, for that He had accomplished, but in the announcing of it, was going to mean He would have me go "a little further" too. *But don't you think I've gone too far already?* I asked God. *I've made such a fool of myself in this whole business.*

Two days later the police officer called and summoned me once more to his office. Showing me John's lengthy record, he then began to shout at me—again. Though considerably intimidated, I reiterated my grand conviction that God could change anybody, given a chance and the time to do it. "After all," I reminded him, "John had only had a brief ten minutes' changing time before the event in question!" Wincing in anticipation of some more verbal spankings, I was not a little surprised when none were forthcoming, and there followed instead a pregnant silence that made me feel most apprehensive.

"So you think God can change anyone, do you?" the policeman asked at last. Before I had time to respond, he shot out an astonishing question, "Even a pigheaded old man of the force like me?" Was he serious, I wondered, or was this just a rhetorical question? Did he really want the answer to that one? I clutched the edge of the desk and invited him to find out for himself. "And just how do I do that, young lady?" he inquired gently. I could see that he was in earnest. He really wanted to know. I couldn't believe it. Fleetingly wondering if it was an offense to lead a policeman to Christ while he was on duty, I plunged in "a little further," and that gruff, bombastic man clambered right into the still point with me, whistle, truncheon, and all.

Years later he was to give a thief a run for his money and lose his leg in the chase, ending up in a Liverpool hospital, where he boldly shared his faith in the Christ he had come to love. The young nurse who cared for him through that amputation, and who told me of the help he was to others around him, was Ann, and it was she who was just about to walk into my life.

One day, having recently joined a church and started a meeting for teenagers, my attention was caught by a young teenage girl. I noticed that she had the considerable interest of every red-blooded male in the room. *It must be hard to be as pretty as that,* I thought, watching the flutterings of the group acknowledging her arrival—*but then that ain't never been my problem! To have the full attention of every masculine eye should be rather gratifying,* I mused as I sang the hymn, my mind not on the words at all—*or would it really be?*

As I teased her after the meeting about the distraction she had caused, I found myself immediately comfortable with her. Entering that girl's heart was like being introduced to springtime. Her life was fresh, sweet, delicate, and clean, ready for the maturing of the summer sun. There was a spiritual edge in evidence that cut away some of the boys' less spiritual and more fleshly wonderings and exposed them to a whole, unspoiled, and well-kept personality, cleaned by grace and helped by love, to guard the boundaries of right from wrong's tramplings. I'd looked into big brown eyes before, but none so luminous as these.

I learned that she was an only child, but that God had matched her with *His* company that led her loneliness to clap its hands and be content. I told her I'd often thought a brother would be nice. Adoring my sister had not prevented me from envying friends with one of each. "Jesus is our elder brother," she commented simply. Autumn wisdom colored her words, and I wondered if the tints of all the seasons of the year were represented in her personality. I was to learn that winter lay ahead.

I discovered that her maturity was a direct result of her home situation. Her mother was an invalid, and the pressure of this burden on the slight shoulders of an only daughter had forced her to grow up. It was a rugged situation and a lonely path for a young teenager to tread. Finding a poem that spoke to her need, I mailed it to her, little knowing it would arrive the week her mother died. It said—

> *I am leading my child to the Heavenly land*
> *I am guiding her day by day*
> *And I ask her now as I take her hand*
> *To come home by a rugged way.*
> *It is not a way she herself would choose*
> *For its beauty she cannot see*
> *But she knows not what her soul would lose*
> *If she trod not that path with Me.*

God had brought us close together for "such a time as this," and seeking to provide some healing activity, I encouraged her to take a part in the teenage leadership of the youth work.

She soon became the brightest spark in a room full of firecrackers, and the explosiveness of the teen potential began to trouble not a few of the more staid members of our congregation. The view from the pew was duly relayed to us: we were to toe the line, run the race—not the race that was set before us, but the one that had already been run by everyone else. "Christian teens should be seen and not heard," I was informed by parents whose children were neither heard nor seen, as they had taken off behind their parents' "church" backs, to enjoy the very world their guardians sought to shield them from. I learned "the world" was a term used for anything outside the church program. The idea was to keep the kids so busy with "churchianity" they would not have breath left for anything else.

It was these young people who were still being compelled and propelled churchward that I was most concerned about. Did God really intend them to roost in the rafters of ecclesiastical stone and organ pipes every day of the week? I read in the Eternal's Law the words: "I was glad when they said unto me, Let us go into the house of the Lord," and I reckoned the man who uttered these pretty sentiments would not have enjoyed our church youth program. Most of the bored church kids who belonged to the church board were secretly mouthing different sentiments to me. They were saying, "I was sad [or even mad] when they said unto me, Let us go into the house of the Lord."

To toe the line—I was cautioned—meant to keep well behind the rope of respectability. "Why can't the young people just be happy to be 'there' in physical bulk?" the hierarchy wondered. Where their minds happened to be parked didn't seem to concern anyone at all. I was finding out that teenagers could very easily learn to send their bodies to worship and leave their emotions in bed, their minds at the movies, and their wills with their "wants" as they dreamed about their future emancipation. Soon they would be too old for Sunday school, and then they would escape to join the rest of their invisible beings, which were already living in "the world."

Something must be done. But what? Was it a program or rather a principle the youth needed to be committed to? Could the Law of the Eternal instruct me in this matter? I read about Peter getting out of the boat on Galilee. Seeing the picture vividly in my mind's eye, I seemed to read the name of our church on the front of that tossing bark. The faces of the eleven disciples reminded me of the faces of our church leadership, and I knew I was like Peter, trying to get out of the boat and do the thing that hadn't been done before. I needed courage to walk the waves and to take the teenagers along with me. We had to get out of the program and into the wild world, testing and trusting His grand ability to keep us afloat.

Did the Bible teach separation from sin or isolation from sinners? It certainly would have been a lot less trouble to accept the oar of conformity, stick with the majority, and toil ahead getting nowhere. That would have required no faith at all. Remembering that Jesus got out of

His boat, leaving the Pharisees to the storm of their controversies in their traditional ship, I knew it was time to hop over the side. When the waves of wounding words and the contrary winds of criticism began to blow, it was awfully hard to keep my eyes on Christ.

Those gusty gales of gossip met me every time I stepped into that church. "It has never been done before. She'll sink, you'll see; it's not scriptural. Whoever heard of anyone trying to walk on water? She can risk her neck if she likes, but I don't see why my child should go down with her."

"Don't listen or look at anything else but Me," commanded Christ. "I bid you come and I'll empower you, walk and I'll walk with you, and even if the worst happens and you sink—I'll put out My hand and fish you out." As I read, marked, and learned the principles, I knew the youth would buy it. A challengeless Christianity would be endured until it could be discarded, but adventure on the high seas would make them disciples forever.

The principles brought the program to birth and I shared it with Ann, who mixed it up with her own sixteen-year-old visions and dreams, and encouraged me to go ahead. I couldn't have done it without her spark, which ignited that lively bunch of firecrackers and set them all jumping. We told the group that classes would commence on how to give away their faith, as, funny enough, that was the only way they would keep it. "Where will we go?" they asked with trepidation.

"We'll go wherever the kids are," we answered. "They'll be in the movie house. In cinemas frighteningly open to the 'slop' of love served up American-style. We can pay our way in, wait for the intermission, and then talk to couples about love God-style instead.

"We'll go and find them in the parks, where grandpa plays bowls on Tuesdays and on Thursdays. The teens will be there too, you'll see," we told them. "They'll be playing a different game from grandpa; they'll be picking up a partner at the tennis courts, dropping him at the golf green, and giggling in the snack shop.

"We'll go down to the sand hills then, where the River Mersey slides against the tangled grass. Those humps and bumps make perfect race courses for all those motorbike fiends who roar in arrogance about our streets.

"We'll find them late at night outside the fish-and-chip shops, licking salty lips.

"And then we'll go and meet them in their coffee bars and pool halls. Maybe we'll even make our own 'pad' and ask the kids we reach to come and let us get to know them there."

Can you just imagine the "splash" as we all jumped out of the boat together? Motivate then mobilize, said the church book on how to keep and interest youth. We found that mobilizing first would motivate far better. In other words, doing what we said was a whole lot more energizing than saying what we'd do.

It was wild adventure. We needn't have worried about doing it "wrong" because nobody had done it before to set a precedent. Our team was met with friendly "Lilipudlian" humor, some suspicious stares, and hilarious leading questions such as: "And what 'abomination' do you lot belong to?" (He meant denomination, of course.) Hiring a room outside the staid church precincts (so as not to turn prospective young people off), we fished the streets and bars and contacted the "Jukebox Jury" crowd, who hung around to pass their judgments on the latest hits. We suggested they come down the road where they wouldn't have to pay for their coffee, and surprise, surprise, they came. Was it going to be as easy as this? Apparently it was.

Vital adolescent life unable to keep still for more than half a minute ebbed and flowed like spring tide through that room. The batches of self-conscious boys and the gaudy, giggling girls readily admitted their lives were void of meaning and that their deepest questionings had only raised more searching screams for help. And then the gangs that roamed the streets and bombed sites of our cities came in. Their "generals" were self-appointed strongmen, bedecked in "leather" uniforms and hung with shiny "braids" of white chrome chains. The visual impact said, "Watch it, I'm tough; try me, I'll win; push me if you dare, and you'll be sorry." Those chains upon their backs and sometimes wrapped around their fists were symbols to Ann and me of their spiritual confinement. I couldn't help thinking of the verse of a hymn I had learned at Cambridge that said—

> *My chains fell off*
> *My heart was free*
> *I rose, went forth*
> *And followed Thee.*

But would such fierce-looking youth really want to hear about a power that would "loose them and let them go"? We wondered about that. The leader of one of the gangs gave me his flick knife as a token of his esteem, and I thanked him profusely, feeling six feet tall. What love was this that pushed and pressured my affections to reach these children playing men?

"What sort of nuts are you anyway to give away free coffee?" asked one of them. If it didn't cost anything, they reckoned it mustn't be any good or else we must be nutty to give it. We used that one to talk about the fact that things that cost some people nothing to receive had sometimes cost the giver a great deal.

That quite naturally led to the story of the cost to the Eternal, who had but one Son, to give Him into the hands of men who would torture Him to death. They were moved. We told them about Jesus and His "gang" of revolutionaries who turned their world upside down. "Actually they turned it right side up!" a quiet "church mouse" muttered into his coffee. He had been sitting next to me, hardly able to believe his ears, watching those wildly dressed teenagers. He had been thinking that no one would ever guess they would even be interested in spiritual things. But then his mind had wandered to some of the people who went to church. He'd heard a preacher quip that some went there to "close their eyes, but others went to eye the clothes." That night he learned for himself that outward appearances really mean nothing very much, for "man looketh on the outward appearance, but the Lord looketh on the heart."

He voiced his thoughts out loud with great fervor and a sudden birth of understanding. One of the gang inquired sarcastically, "You all right, mate?" He laughed out loud and began to articulate his faith, drawing small, precise word pictures that the group could easily grasp. We gazed at him in absolute amazement. Our small church mouse had been transformed by "war" into a mighty lion shaking his mane fiercely in the face of the opposition.

The next night the Bible class was packed to the rafters. Never had we had such interest in the text. I peppered all I taught with illustrations from the night before. Some cowardly souls who had been waiting to see what would happen to those who'd ventured forth signed up for the next "raid." Those who had been out on the streets stayed late seeking answers to questions they had been asked and had not been able to answer. They couldn't wait to get out to the "battle" again, this time armed with "give away" Bibles. We were not a little encouraged to find them gratefully received, though some of the takers couldn't even read.

"I had a Bible once," a red-haired boy informed us proudly, fingering his gift, "and it wasn't just any old Bible," he added hastily. "It was one of them there 'holy' ones." One of his friends believed a "holy" Bible belonged in church, and it was just the "unholy" ones that were sold in the shops. This led to a "groupie" girl asking us if we'd take her and her friends along to see what "church" was really like. Ann and I looked at each other, conjuring up mental pictures of a most alarming nature. Chickening out, we decided to take them downtown to an old Anglican church where no one knew us. The date was set, and off we went. Punctuality not being a gang characteristic, we arrived when the service was nearly over, which was just as well, as it turned out.

We had hoped the Anglo "catholic" ritual and aesthetic atmosphere would subdue their spirits—but unfortunately it didn't. Putting their feet up on the pews in front of them, our "worshipers" lit their cigarettes, reckoning it must be all right seeing there seemed to be quite a bit of smoke about. One of the girls commented in a loud voice that the board at the front of the church had numbers on it that reminded her of the "odds at the dogs." (She meant the greyhound races.)

The priest was valiantly struggling to complete his sermon, and I noticed that the leader of our gang was trying to set the behavior pattern for his group by leaning forward and listening intently. Suddenly, to my horror, and I may add the shock of the priest, he shot up out of his seat to ask a question. Actually it was a very good question, and I would ordinarily have been very proud of him, if I hadn't been trying to look like a hymnbook in the rack in front of me.

Losing interest in the proceedings, two more of our first-time churchgoers got up and began to rummage through the implements at the back of the church, looking for goodness knows what. The priest, having recovered some of his composure, hastily descended from his high place and proceeded—nay cantered—toward the pilferers. He was intoning a "beefed-up" canticle to keep time with his busy feet, and was preceded by a hurried-up little man robed most royally and swinging a pot of incense. The boy whose loud question still hung unanswered in the air rose in brotherly concern. He could see what was happening. He wasn't stupid. It was obvious the leader of the priest's "gang" was in trouble, and gang leaders have a camaraderie few but them understand. Feeling very magnanimous, he decided to offer help. "Hey, missus," he called out, "yer handbag's on fire!" Church was finished, and so, needless to say, was I. Our "bunch" had proved to be a long way from being transformed into Sunday morning worshipers, just as the Sunday morning worshipers had proved themselves a long way from being ready for our bunch.

Undaunted, some of the gang volunteered to help us reach the ones they said "really" needed religion. We accepted their offer and set about picking up the teenage drunks who fell into the gutters late at night after the pubs were closed. We'd try to find out where they lived and take them home or down to the Chinese Gospel Mission, where we had been helping renovate the premises. Then we would walk down to the notorious area behind Lime Street Station, a black web of pimps, waiting like monstrous spiders for some female teenage flies.

We were glad of our boys' company. "Teddy" boys, so called because they emulated "Edwardian"-style dress, roamed looking for a fight. Policemen went about in threes with trained Alsatian dogs to keep these young thugs under control. The "Teds" responded by training their own mongrel soldiers, keeping them starved to add some "extra bite" to their attacks. It was very scary. Talk about being out of our depth! But then, we found no experts walking on that water. All of us out there were getting pretty wet as we learned everything the hard way. I remembered my headmistress's command to "leave the mothers to her," and I began to know what it was to bank on my Divine Headmaster drawing a chalk line across our path, saying with heavenly authority to our antagonists, "Thus far and no farther!" This time I was not facing irritated moms with their umbrellas, but "Teds" and their much more lethal sticks of war.

I learned like Daniel that praying regularly three times a day did not exempt me from the lions' den, but then He never promised that it would! He didn't say, "I'll save you from the den of lions," but rather, "I'll save you *in* it, revealing some aspect of Myself that you could never have known or 'seen' from the safety of your prayer chamber." I found a poster and stuck it up on my wall to remind me of these things. It said, "A ship in the harbor is safe—but then, that's not what ships are for!"

Down at the Chinese mission, I was overjoyed to meet an old schoolmate of mine whom my family knew well. She had recently become a believer. I was especially pleased because my parents were becoming understandably alarmed with all the strange new company I was keeping and with my rather risky extracurricular activities. I was sure they would be a lot less apprehensive if they knew Joyce was working with us. It did help a bit—until she married the missionary in charge, who was Chinese, and *that* didn't help at all.

We met a downtown pastor who was filling a most unusual pulpit down at the Pier Head by the ferries that chugged back and forth across the Mersey. The dockers, office workers, and visitors mingled for their lunch break, and our pastor friend simply turned an orange box upside down and showed us how to get a crowd, hold a crowd, and touch a crowd—even a crowd of "hard hat" dockers out for a lark.

There for a while, those laborers, talking tough about their "capitalist" foes in Whitehall, ringed him round, belligerently challenging his premises. "Try keeping this lot interested," our intrepid friend remarked, "and you'll soon find out if you have a preaching gift or not." We assured him we were quite sure we *didn't* have one, to which he replied, "How do you know—have you ever tried?" Horror-struck at the very idea, we stood there shaking our heads.

It was time for him to begin. The crowd gathered as he got up on his orange box and began to joke and kid them. We listened with awe as he deftly caught the hecklers' words, wrapped them around with earthy wisdom and clever applications of the Truth, and threw them back hard at his challengers. One little man was a regular. He was called "Cheeky Charlie" and prided himself on being a prize heckler. The crowd loved it when the pastor and Cheeky Charlie locked horns, and they would gather to enjoy the entertainment. That day the sermon was about Christ knocking at the door of our hearts. "The Bible says we have to let Him in," said the preacher. This was too much for Charlie, who rudely interrupted to point out he thought that was stupid, as he didn't see how Jesus could live in anyone's heart. Hadn't he just passed a butcher shop and seen a heart hanging there? Why, the heart was just a blood pump, so how on earth could Jesus live in it?

"Are you married, Charlie?" inquired our friend. Taken off his guard, Charlie replied that he was.

"Did you ever do any courting before you got wed?" was the next question.

"Well, yes," muttered Charlie, now becoming somewhat bewildered at the turn of the conversation.

"Did you ever take your sweetheart for a walk in the silvery moonlight, gaze into her eyes, and say, 'Darling, I love you with all my blood pump'?" The crowd roared approval, Charlie hastily disappeared, and the pastor explained that our heart was a term used in the Bible to describe the seat of our emotions—our innermost being and the place that Christ desired to live.

He turned to us as we stood there in awe at the whole proceeding. I gasped as he gave a very authoritative order—"Jill, come here and tell these people what a difference it made when you let Jesus come into your heart." Somehow I did as I was told and added a few sentences to his comments, wondering how on earth my words could have any relevance to those people. The pastor had been born and raised among them and so fully understood where they were coming from. How could my testimony mean anything when I hadn't had such a background? The meeting was over and our friend thanked me for my words and commented, "A witness like yours illustrates the Truth I have been preaching. You were saying in effect, 'It's real, it worked in my life.' You don't need to be a 'docker' to win a docker for Christ, you know," he continued, apparently reading my thoughts. "Our ministry would be very limited if we could only speak to the people 'like us.' We are told to preach the Gospel—not our own experience. It's God's Word that will do the trick, but it helps to put 'windows' into our teaching to let people 'see into' the Truth, and that's what a testimony can do."

Here was a man we could admire and learn from. A man who knew what it was to trust God and pay the cost of walking fearlessly among the men and the Teddy boys alike. He would take his big, worn Bible and go among the warring factions, with nothing but his faith in God to protect him. His sheer guts and courage earned him the grudging respect of the gangs he tried to reach. Slowly and surely one here and one there came to know the pastor's God.

Repercussions were inevitable. One night a gang member who was very angry that his leader had come to Christ and turned in his weapons at the police station decided to teach "that preacher guy" a lesson. Breaking the top off a bottle, he put the jagged neck in his pocket and made his way to our friend's house. Warned by some miraculous alert system, the pastor opened his door, put out his hand, and hauled the fellow inside. Grasping the boy's wrist, he pulled the boy's hand from his deep pocket and with it the broken glass intended for his eyes. "Come on in then," he chaffed the boy, "and I'll give you a teat for your bottle!" Tough and tender, tried and true, God took this young minister and filled his life with power till soon his church was filled with the most extraordinary creatures you could find anywhere.

Visiting his worship service one Sunday, Ann and I sat among the strangest set of people imaginable. One of them insisted on cleaning his nails with his flick knife the whole time, while a most respectable-looking gentleman on his left, who appeared to be completely at ease, shared his Bible with him. This touched me very deeply, for I realized we had not found a church full of "weirdos" but a place where people gathered from every conceivable walk of life. There were mothers and fathers and children with "no way out" marks written on their faces, and suddenly I had an intense longing for this to happen in our church too. Maybe there *were* some adults back home in the suburbs who would be willing to welcome our own wild group of teenagers. Surely this was what church was all about. Not peer groups "peering" around in suspicion at anyone who wasn't like them, but people who didn't conform and people who did, loving and serving the Lord together.

Could Christ cross those barriers and make the world sit up and take notice? He had crossed the age gulf for Ann and me, and He'd done it for both of us across the cultural gap with our young people. Could He do it across the class barrier as well? That night I read the confirmation I was looking for. "In Christ there is neither Jew nor Greek, bond nor free, male nor female—but, all are *one* in Christ Jesus."

Within one short week a deacon and his wife had opened their hearts and their home to us and soon began to change my mind about our church. They convinced me that everybody in our congregation wasn't sitting in the boat, but there was a little justified apprehension at the dangers we were exposing their young folk to. The biggest thing they did for me was to change the course of that youth ministry by lending some wisdom and help, prayer support, and influence back in our fellowship. They taught me that the church was Christ's body and there was no way I could be excited about my Lord's Head without being equally enthralled with the rest of His body. It was this man who encouraged us to bring our young people "in."

The story of the impact of that invasion is best summed up by a poem my future husband was to write about a practically identical situation in our own congregation some years later:

> *All These Kids in Church?*
> How would you explain it?
> The latest fad?
> An emotional upheaval?
> Communist infiltration?
> Spiritual revival?

Ann

All those kids in church!
Unashamed,
Unabashed,
Undismayed,
Unbelievable!
Listening,
Learning,
Loving,
Yearning.
Togetherness
Foreverness
Warm smiles,
Quiet eyes,
Serene expression,
Deep impression.
Sharing,
Caring,
Bearing,
Daring,
But where are the old folks?
Some with
Bowed head,
Faces red,
Fled!
Some dismayed,
Afraid,
Prayed and
Stayed.
Knees shaking,
Hearts breaking,
Efforts making,
Chances taking,
To believe,
To receive,
To achieve,

To relieve.
Willing,
Watching,
Waiting,
Worrying,
Saints.
White hair,
Long hair,
No hair,
Tinted hair
Bowed
In prayer.
Weeping together,
Reaping together,
Sowing together,
Growing together.
Lord's work,
Team work.
Worship,
Fellowship,
Relationship,
Stewardship,
Discipleship.
One body,
One Spirit,
One hope,
One Lord,
One faith,
One baptism,
One God,
One Father
Above them all,
Through them all,
And in them all,
AMEN.

It was some of these dear folks who
"stayed"

Knees shaking,
  Hearts breaking,
    Efforts making,
      Chances taking,

that told us about Capernwray Hall, a Christian Holiday Center for young people. "You should take our young people there," they suggested to Ann and me. "There is so much value in getting them away from their unhelpful environment for a while." They told us they would help us with the money that we would need. It sounded like a fabulous place and a great idea. "We'll go," we said. And we did.

To Be a Friend:
Application and Journal

....

1. How comfortable are you in crossing age, cultural, class, or racial barriers to form friendships? What aspects of such potential friendships make you uncomfortable?

2. Who do you have in your life from outside your normal categories of friends who might become a friend? For example, does a teenage girl in your church watch you with admiration or seek you out for conversation?

3. What areas of ministry could be a good area for teamwork with someone different from you?

4. In your interest in being separate from sin, do you find yourself isolated from sinners? If you interact regularly with unbelieving neighbors or coworkers, how can you "go a little further" to influence them for Christ? If your personal contacts are almost exclusively with believers, what can you change in your life?

....

For Action:
Tell one other person about any area in which you feel Christ's prompting to "go a little further." Ask her to come back to you in a month to ask about your progress in that area.

....

Chapter Six

....

Joan

....

*A*fter we tumbled out of "Ben Hur's Chariot," as the Capernwray bus was affectionately named, Major W. I. Thomas, D.S.O.T.D., introduced himself to us. "This is our home," he said, waving his hand in the direction of the castle; "enjoy it!" He cracked a couple of jokes, clipped two of the kids playfully over the ears, rolled up his sleeves, and disappeared down a trench some German boys were furiously digging. "It's a shame w'ot these geezers 'ave come to," muttered one of our mob. "Own a castle they do, but 'ave to do all the work themselves!"

"The Major believes in a Christianity that isn't afraid to get its hands dirty," explained a boy who greeted us. "Those letters after his name, D.S.O.T.D., represent military honors for bravery in World War II." He paused and grinned ruefully—going on to say, "Those of us on staff think they should also stand for 'Dirty Shirt On, Tinkering Down Drains!'" The kids, observing the flying shovels and hearing the guttural German banter in the trench, decided they liked the look and the sound of *the Major.*

"'Is house isn't so bad either," hissed another city kid, gaping aloft at the carved stone faces leering down at him from the cornice of the roof.

"What are them gargles doing up there?" asked a boy very importantly. He wanted everyone to know he knew the name.

"Gargoyles, stupid," a rather intelligent kid with thick glasses corrected him.

Gazing at the emerald green panorama of the English countryside, I was caught by some moments of nostalgia, realizing we were but a few miles away from my wartime refuge. The spell was broken by a city girl's impatient query, "Well, where's the nearest Woolworth's then?" *Woolworth's!* Could there be no real happiness or sense of security for a town teen without Woolworth's? Gazing around at God's canvas brushed with spring colors, tempered with the soft sweet kisses of the summer rain, I almost thought of *town* as a dirty word, and I breathed a silent prayer on behalf of our concrete city hermits. Would they dare to venture out of their sealed conceptions, to smell the damp, dark musk of perfumed leaves and hear the whispered wisdom of God's works, audible at last without the thunder of a thousand tons of metropolitan machinery?

My reverie was interrupted by a sudden splash, and I made a hurried mental note to ban our youngsters from the lily pond nestled like some decorated navel in a tummy of rose beds. "Get out of there," I shouted, and, "let's go—"

Racing up to the top of the steps, they were met by the croquet lawn rolled out in splendid decorum. *Hmm,* I thought, picturing the "upper class" game being murdered by "lower class" mortals such as we. That's all we needed—our gang let loose with croquet mallets.

"Oooo-eee," squealed a bunch of girls who had climbed up the stone spiral stairs to the top of the tower. Lilliputian against the sky, they were busy pretending to throw each other over the edge. At least I *hoped* they were only pretending. Some of our more hungry hooligans came skidding around the corner to tell us they had discovered the "Beehive" coffee shop, so called, they had been told, because you could buy sweet things there and "get stung." A wrestling match ensued, and Ann and I gave up on them, escaping indoors where we made our way to our room and proceeded to get ready for the meeting.

Spice and variety in the shape of Europe's youth packed the lecture hall, the medley of languages coaxed into harmony by the insistent vibrant call of the guitar. Hundreds of young throats opened at full throttle assured more timid vocalists that the God who is Eternal Youth enjoys the noise of praise. The music made a highway in the mind for the vehicle of words in the Major's pungent talk. His preaching spoke to the crux of the matter. Our matter! Oh joy. Fancy finding yourself impatient for the next time you could go to church!

Late at night, leaders were assigned to take devotions. Our leader had that "much loved" look about her. She kept smiling lots of secret little smiles that we just knew were the result of things she'd been let in on straight from heaven. We couldn't wait for her to pass them on to us. Piled in happy heaps upon a few protesting beds, with nighties hugged around their bony knees and shiny eyes lit up with bright expectancy, those special, special children we had brought to this special place rapped about the Law of the Eternal. We marveled at raw wisdom that cut cant and insisted on being relevant.

Some bereft of love relationships back home leaned heavily on a newfound Friend, soaking up the permeating atmosphere of Christ's concern. Tousled heads of hair hung over Bible texts spread open on laps as the kids struggled to make sense of the outdated English. "W'ot's it mean—'he that hath ears to hear, let him hear'?" asked one. "That's easy—'pin yer lugs back,'" supplied the next. And then, "W'ot's an epistle—the wife of an apostle?" And on to deeper wonderings about the lack of power showing a strange inconsistency in some lives that had been given to God.

"What does it really mean to backslide?" pursued a quiet, earnest "straight" kid. "Is it possible to actually slip out of God?" Our leader answered that it wasn't and that the word used for backsliding in the Scriptures really meant to back hold or hold back, and we could *all* relate to that.

Devotions over, the pillow fights began, with frantic shrieking at the puffy blows. The stubbed toes of the chased drew cries that were apparently piercing enough to summon the cool, calm—but most collected and commanding—voice of *Mrs. Major*. "Quiet down now, girls," she said in such a way that the "arguments" went straight to bed and so did we.

Lying still at last, thinking about that huge house fashioned so ideally for the job God had in mind, I thought about the people who must have lived here in the past. How surprised they would be to visit us and find twenty-five girls in their boudoir. What must it have been like to live in the lap of such luxury? One family in all this space!

Rising early the next morning, Ann and I toured the building, discovering the paneled study and elegant dining halls overlooking flower beds that sported a profusion of perfection in the shape of the English rose. There were huge marble fireplaces and a somber, giant hallway with the graceful wooden balustrade reminding us of so many proud soldiers standing at attention saluting Europe's youth.

While walking along the stone-flagged corridors, we discovered the servants' quarters. The handmaidens of old served their master diligently behind the scenes and were never allowed past a certain respected boundary. We discovered these ancient pantries were still the *servants'* quarters—this time scenes of diligent Christian servitude, but with one *major,* or I should say *Mrs. Major,* difference. The mistress of the house was discovered down upon her knees—not in supplication, but in irrigation. The drain had clogged up. She smiled serenely, refusing to interpret our presence as an intrusion into forbidden territory, but rather as an opportunity to take an interest in us. Disengaging herself from the battle of the u-bend, she straightened up and talked us into a mighty good feeling of importance by inviting our involvement in the bread pantry. Cutting up sandwiches with Mrs. Major, or Joan as I came to know her, suddenly became the most *queenly* occupation possible.

The sliced bread was waiting, set in stacks that looked like mini replicas of the leaning tower of Pisa. We wondered how slapping slices of pressed beef squarely on bread or gluing it together with tangy marmalade could give us such an unusual sense of purpose. We supposed it was the unexpected privilege of being shut up together in such a confined space with the lady boss, who, we soon discovered, didn't think of herself in any such high way at all. In fact, we became increasingly aware she didn't spend much time thinking about herself, peri-od. You could tell by her conversation. Ann and I were suddenly made aware of the *I, me, my,* and *mine* quality of our own side of the dia-logue, and the *Thy, Thou,* and *Thine* side of hers. Not that she talked religious rigmarole—in fact she didn't even mention God. It was just a sort of sweet unself-consciousness that told you she did not consider herself the center and circumference of her own world. I was grateful to the bread for offering us such an opportunity.

Moving at a graceful trot, as a thoroughbred should, Joan led us around her pasture, introducing us to the tea pantry (sacred to all old English castles) where stacks of shiny aluminum teakettles waited as if on parade to do battle with the Englishman's insatiable thirst. Next we were taken to the small kitchen, where a windmill of whirling arms washed and wiped the cutlery that was orchestrating tinny tunes of joy. "Don't you have any washing-up equipment?" I gasped.

"You're looking at it," Joan responded cheerfully, patting the smil-ing girls on the shoulders. It was plain to see these youngsters were having a great deal of fun doing a menial task in a genial way for God—and Joan, of course.

There was obviously nothing she expected these servants to do that she had not first done herself or that they had not done together. Yet, as we watched her in the coming days, we became convinced she wasn't being a martyr—she was simply doing her many duties because she honestly believed they were the very chores the Lord Jesus wanted *her* to do for Him. Up to now I had always thought of any physical task that cropped up in my leadership role as a necessity so that I might *show an example* to those under me. But here we were intro-duced to an altogether different quality of leadership. Here was an au-thority whose example portrayed an *attitude of gratitude.* Joan ran that center on these terms: "Let's do this for Him, and let's do it together. I'll do the hardest and the most mundane part of it—*not* to save you from doing it, but because *I want* to take the burden of the duty as part of *my* love gift to the Lord."

Joan surely knew what the "Order of the Towel" was all about. The dirty feet were no sooner still than the bowl of water and her glad hands were there to wipe them clean. How long was it going to take, I wondered as I rattled the cutlery in the silver pantry, measured the tea in the tea pantry, and slapped on the corned beef in the bread pantry, till I could serve my God like that without needing an audience or a fanfare? How many years would my *out back* training take before God could ever trust me up front?

Each afternoon at four o'clock, the entire conference crammed together in the lounge for teatime. It would have been nice to meet outside on the lawn, but as Major put it, the *liquid sunshine* prevented us from doing so. The raisin-eyed scones lying meekly among our sandwiches seemed to watch with justified apprehension the approach of hundreds of chattering, bright, white teeth intent on gobbling them up.

Ann and I helped to collect the dirty dishes. On the floor by the side of a seemingly very small cup and saucer sat a very large, handsome Englishman. Doing my knee-bend act for the umpteenth time and rising with my pouch full of crockery like some ungainly kangaroo, I traveled past a pair of broad shoulders and an intriguing mouth shaped in the widest, whitest, cheekiest grin imaginable. Passing by the strong line of his profile, I wondered aghast, *Whatever are my wonderings wondering about?* Arriving at the level of his hazel eyes, I knew! I was electrically acknowledging that slanted, quizzical gaze that said, "Hi, I'm Stuart, and I'd like to know your name."

Flushing deeply at his obvious interest, I completed my lunge upward and, plunking the dishes on the tea tray with an embarrassing crescendo of noise, turned around to take another look. He was patting the floor beside him, inviting me to sit down, and making it look like the only place on earth worth sitting on. Inwardly rebuking my knees, which had rushed to obey, and summoning up every bit of resistance I could, I said, "I'm sorry—but I'm collecting the dishes." Gazing coolly around the lounge, which had no dishes left to collect, he shot me a look as if to say, *What's the matter, little lady? Are you afraid of getting involved?*

Severely lecturing my heart on the senseless stupidity of getting hurt, I reminded myself of my almost certain spinsterhood. What an awful word that is, I thought mournfully—*spinster!* It conjured up a vision of a tall, skinny character in knitted stockings and sensible shoes, peering at her pressed-wildflower collection through intelligent-looking bifocals. Her cat (spinsters always had cats) would have to be trained to drink water instead of milk. You don't have much money to waste when you're a spinster, you know.

These morbid, and incidentally totally unrealistic, thoughts, were rudely interrupted by the very distinctive voice of the big handsome Englishman inquiring if I would like to play a game of table tennis. A girl had appeared by his side, I noticed with a certain relief mixed with an infuriating sense of disappointment. I shouldn't be surprised to see some female company, I told myself. Judging him to be about twenty-five, it would have been a highly unusual thing to find him on the loose when he looked as good as he did.

As we walked toward the game room, he began to tease me as if he'd known me all his life. *"Down Upsey,"* I commanded my emotions sternly, but they appeared neither to hear nor understand. What on earth was happening? Was God teasing me—or was the devil using this man as a temptation to divert me from my spiritual goals? How could a poor girl like me know if all this was from the devil or the Lord? He didn't *look* as though he was from the devil—in fact he looked good enough to eat—but *that* was where all the trouble had started in the first place. The devil wasn't stupid enough to offer Eve a rotten apple. Anyway, I concluded, he was probably married with at least three kids.

The problem was we weren't talking about apples, and I soon discovered the girl who was with him was just an acquaintance, and he wasn't married at all . . . and all at once, I found myself hoping against hope this craggy-looking Englishman would not notice the effect he was having upon me. His hair, fingering the back of his collar, invited me to touch it and tuck it into place, and I wondered if he realized how his masculinity had reached out so boldly to match my need.

Somehow I knew he was daring me to venture forth around the barricade I'd built to save my heart from harm. Ping, pong, ping, pong, said the ball. That white blob appeared to lace us together with invisible strings of attachment that surprised us both with joy.

Two days later, it was time to go home. Brushing my dreams with color, Stuart Briscoe asked me for my address. By this time I knew he was a banker who traveled and used this opportunity to preach and teach in youth groups and churches, but I was again taken by surprise when he casually threw an exciting idea into our final conversation. Maybe he could come and talk to our bunch of youngsters when he came to Liverpool, he suggested. Maybe? Both of us knew it wasn't going to be a *maybe,* both of us knew it *must be a must.* My affected affections peeped timidly out from behind my very proper handshake. He grinned a sort of secret acknowledgment and, touching my face with his eyes, was gone—for a while.

Eighteen happy months later there was no doubt left in either of our minds. We belonged together.

"The Eternal's orders are just, a joy to the heart," Psalm 19 assured us. Convinced *He* had ordered our love relationship and that it was indeed *right,* we heartily agreed and told Him "Thank You," rejoicing in the words of the preacher from the book of Ecclesiastes, who said—

> *Two* are better than one; because they have a good reward for their labour. For if they fall, the one will lift up his fellow: but woe to him that is alone when he falleth; for he hath not another to help him up. Again, if two lie together, then they have heat: but how can one be warm alone? And if one prevail against him, two shall withstand him; and a *threefold cord is not quickly broken.* (Ecclesiastes 4:9–12, italics added)

To us the "threefold cord that is not quickly broken" spoke of the binding blessing of the Lord around our partnership, declaring loudly to the world, "What God has joined together, let no man put asunder."

We were married on July 26—I think—and it was raining—I've been told, and I was scared—*I remember that!* Feeling like Lot's wife, struck into immobility by that fateful look back, I glanced desperately at my mother for help. Observing her younger daughter looking like that frightened pillar of salt, she rose to the occasion.

"God's going to bring you and Stuart together, Jill," she reminded

me sharply. *Shape up,* her tone indicated. *Step out,* her eyes commanded. Spurred on by her loving insistence, I moved—I believe—into the
car . . . I vaguely recollect—with my father—*I do remember that!* We
didn't say one word all the way to the church. Not one. What does a
father think about on such a day?

I longed to break that poignant quiet and thank him for his marvelous care of me, but the silent statement of his lasting love reduced
me to as many raindrops as the splattered windows boasted, and all I
could do was reach out *one more time* for his arm—saying without the
spoiling of a word, one more hour, Dad, just one. One more walk
with me as yours before I leave and cleave forever to another man. I
asked my heavenly Father to tell my earthly one my heart, and I
begged forgiveness for the daughter sins I was suddenly counting. I
wondered if on such a day fathers took a guilt trip of their own among
the *should haves* and the *why didn't I's* of child rearing? If such was the
case, I asked the Eternal to remind us both of the grace of God. Grace
to cover *all* our sin the Bible said, and that meant all my teenage sin
and all my mother sin-to-be and grace, my dearest father, for your father sins as well—although at that moment of time I couldn't think of
one of them. And that's just as it should be, I decided as the spell was
broken and the door swung open to my brand-new life. Helping me
out of the wedding car, Dad laughed with me in relief as we stored our
precious time together in the vault of treasured memories.

In the crowded church I saw that our "gang" had pressed forward.
Their fresh, endearing faces shouted proud attention to their best blue
jeans sported specially for the day. The preacher gave a talk—telling of
the time that Jesus visited a home and drew the inevitable crowd. "It
was noised that Jesus was in the house," he said, then, looking at Stuart and me standing before him, already one in all but flesh, he added,
"So it shall be with your home too." We nodded in glad and full anticipation of his words. *But first the honeymoon!*

What ridiculous fun—but what surprises too. Nobody had told
me. Stuart didn't want me to pick out his ties, which was a real shock.
Didn't all married women get to do that once the vows were vowed?

He didn't seem to appreciate my telling him how to drive either. We were touring the continent of Europe, driving through Switzerland. Having been here with my family when I was fourteen, I was feeling very superior, and I kept up a barrage of most helpful advice on how to drive on the wrong side of the street. Eventually bugging my brand-new husband into letting me have a go, I began to discover it wasn't quite as easy as it looked.

Seeing my confusion, Stuart commenced to give me some staccato commands. I wondered if he usually clung onto the door handle like that when someone else was driving. He appeared to be an extremely nervous passenger. When we entered the city of Berne in Switzerland, the first traffic island loomed on the horizon, and the briefing in my right ear began all over again. "Reverse all driving patterns—watch your right-hand side—remember the cars from subsidiary roads have right-of-way—and—and—*why don't you slow down now and let the old man climb off the hood!*" he ended somewhat desperately.

Adjusting my sights straight ahead, I gazed aghast into an aged gentleman's terrified eyes. Apparently he had endeavored to leap over our vehicle to avoid being knocked under it, and there he was—walking stick and all draped prostrate over the hood clutching the Austin motif on the front of the car. His hat was over his ear and his feet were windmilling around as we careened the wrong way around the traffic island. When I slammed on the brakes, Grandpa shot into some accommodating lady's backside.

"He seems to be all right," Stuart reported after looking back, "but as soon as it's safe, you can *STOP!—and* we'll check it out." It sounded to me as if he didn't mean stop—he meant *abdicate*—but suddenly we found ourselves crossing a river on a high narrow bridge, and there was no place I could stop.

Glancing nervously sidewise for some more instructions, I saw that my spouse's eyes were riveted straight ahead. Intrigued by his super profile, I foolishly gazed at him until, without flickering one riveted eyelash, he whispered in a hoarse voice, "Slow down—Jill, please. . . ."

Boy, what a wreck! I thought. I wouldn't have expected this from an ex-Royal Marine Commando. He was poking his finger feebly at the front window; I followed the direction of his gesture and noticed a little man on a bike immediately in front of our car. He was pedaling so fast his whole body was a jerking jumble of rippling muscles, and his head kept bobbing around at us like a puppet pulled by hundreds of invisible strings. "Wow, what a pace he's going," I commented admiringly. "He must be doing at least thirty miles per hour. Maybe it's a national sport."

"He has no option," Stuart retorted icily. "You've somehow got our bumper under his back wheel guard." We stopped—all of us, Stuart and I and the man on the bike—and it seemed as though our stopping was sort of symbolic. I meekly got out of the car and changed places, and as we continued on our way in a somewhat heavy silence, I began to do a lot of serious thinking. Was marriage to be a continual abdication of my driving rights, I wondered, or was I only expected to yield up my driving wrongs? Were there to be some things a woman was not allowed to do after *the knot* was tied that she had freely done when it was *not a knot?* Somehow I had thought that marriage was *not to be a knot* at all, but a meshing together of two strands of string— making them one smooth, strong piece. But here we were on our honeymoon, already tied in *knobbled knots* of conflict!

Did marriage relegate me forever to the passenger seat, merely reading the map while he drove all the way? Would Stuart be not only the bread winner—but *the only winner?* How could we begin to complement each other instead of competing when both of us had such strong gifts and personalities? Was a Christian wife supposed to wrap up her spiritual gifts and return them to the Sender with one hand while unwrapping the wedding gifts with the other? I didn't know, and I wasn't sure I should even be having such questions on our honeymoon. I decided to wait to ask my husband when we got back home.

One year and one child later, I found myself still struggling with the problem. Was a believing wife meant only to exercise her spiritual abilities *within* her role? And what happened if the gifts didn't fit within the role expected of her? Plenty of people offered advice, but they were folk whose gifts and talents appeared *perfectly role-shaped* to begin with. I thought about Mrs. Major and longed to ask her if she had any trouble conforming while performing. After twelve months of marriage, the chance came to watch my model missionary in action, as Stuart was called to leave business and lend his expertise to the Capernwray staff as treasurer of the fellowship.

It was certainly no small thing for him to resign a fine career, and we asked for clear direction from the Lord. As usual my heart outran my head and I chattered, "You pray, darling—I'll pack." But my level-headed husband herded up my wild reactions and brought them firmly back to the fold of reason. The Eternal's command is clear, said Psalm 19—reminding us that when we need assurance He has promised to provide it. We sought the advice of wise, respected Christian leaders and individually looked for a sense of the right thing to do.

A few days later, after having asked God for specific words of guidance, Stuart was unexpectedly called into conference with the top executives of the bank. Having little time before his interview, he found a quiet spot and opened his New Testament. "Lay not up for yourselves treasures upon earth, where moth and rust doth corrupt, and where thieves break through and steal," he read. "But lay up for yourselves treasures in heaven, where neither moth nor rust doth corrupt, and where thieves do not break through nor steal" (Matthew 6:19–20). Being in the headquarters of a bank, such words were thrown into sharp focus. "Lift up your eyes," said a later text, "and look on the fields; for they are white already to harvest" (John 4:35). Given such directives, it only remained to face those most eminent gentlemen and refuse their marvelous offer of promotion, accepting instead the *high calling* of the Christian ministry.

Once the decision was made, all sorts of confirmation followed. God had promised us we would hear a voice behind us saying, "This is the way, walk ye in it," and we came to understand that the voice was behind us because we were moving ahead in the right direction. Encouragements followed daily, culminating in a relevant letter from Stuart's mother. She had just lost her husband and was feeling very lonely. Capernwray was within driving distance of her home, and how advantageous our move would be for her. The very morning that letter arrived, our reading centered around the last words of the Lord Jesus from the cross to His mother, "Woman, behold thy son," and to John, "Behold thy mother."

A few weeks later, on a cold winter's night, as Stuart sat hunched up warming his toes in front of a small electric fire in a chilly hotel room, he knew the time had come to write that final letter of resignation. "Confirm this just once more, Father," he prayed as he sealed the letter and opened his Bible. He read of Peter in prison and of the angel who said to him, "Arise up quickly. . . . Gird thyself, and bind on thy sandals. . . . Cast thy garment about thee, and follow me"—and so he did, said the Word concerning Peter. Somehow Stuart knew it was a word to his own heart as well.

We went to Capernwray from the prison of winter as springtime began to applaud the miracle of birth. Both of us had kept a verse of Scripture relating to the move to share with each other, and when we reached Capernwray, I read mine to Stuart from the book of Isaiah— "For ye shall go out with joy, and be led forth with peace: the mountains and the hills shall break forth before you into singing, and all the trees of the field shall clap their hands!" (Isaiah 55:12).

He gave me a strange look as I asked him what the particular promise was that God had given to him. "It's the same one," he said quietly. "That is the very verse that God impressed upon my spirit as well."

Settling in and turning our attention to the business of *being* the missionaries we had become, I began to wonder all over again about my role. Looking at the structure of the mission, I commented to Stuart that it didn't appear to be the accepted thing for a woman to be up front teaching and preaching. "Just because it hasn't been done in the past," he answered, "doesn't mean it won't be accepted in the future. But," he went on, "why don't you start practicing your gifts where they are needed most and where you've proved them before—outside Capernwray's boundaries."

Oh Lord, not again, I groaned. Here I was busy trying to be submissive to my husband, who was supposed to be sheltering me under the umbrella of his protection, and all he did was cheerfully hold it over my head while he pushed me out into the rain.

And so I began to reach out to the neighborhood, hoping rain-drops would be the only things that fell on my head. An outreach like the one I had in mind had not been attempted before, but to my great relief and delight Joan was the first to encourage me in the venture.

Stuart's abilities became evident, and Major generously worked out a three-month preaching trip to the United States for him. I wasn't quite sure if I was ready for the repercussions of that tour, guessing—as it happened, quite rightly—that more and more opportunities would open up to him as a result. How was I expected to exercise my gifts within my role in the absence of my role maker? How could the orders of the Lord be altogether right when it meant my doing with-out a husband and the children without a father?

I looked around for some relief but saw only other lonely mission-ary wives either playing martyr or looking as though they did not feel any sense of loss at all. Joan herself didn't see Major for months on end, and that had been the pattern for years. Stuart suggested I talk to her about it, but how could the novice ever face the expert and admit she'd failed before she'd hardly begun? I was sure she would hit me over the head with some tried and true Bible verse and send me on my way with my tail between my legs.

Eventually, the situation became so serious I had to go anyway. I will never forget leaning against the door of her office watching her read a pile of important-looking letters. She was a truly beautiful woman with short, naturally wavy black hair, a clear complexion, and the most direct gaze possible. Her Irish heritage had lent her that zany, saving sense of fun that searched for the humor of the thing, even if it was as small and insignificant as a needle in a haystack. She would burrow into a problem and search diligently till she came up with a laugh from the recesses of the biggest, heaviest stack of hay a horse ever had to carry. This time her search would be fruitless, I decided. I was *long* past laughing at loneliness.

Pushing aside the pile of letters to give me the full benefit of her attention, she found me rehearsing my part of hurt heroine, dramati-cally declaring it was most unfair of the men to expect us to carry the load at home while they flew around the world giving their little speeches. Smiling her sweet Irish smile and seeming to be content to wait for her cue, she so disarmed me that I forgot my lines. Turning to my bitter self as prompter, I found him fled and honesty holding the script instead. *"I'm bitter, hurt, and lonely,"* I burst out, *"and I want my husband!"* It was said. Marching around that little office the words clattered their noisy way into her quiet understanding and were given grave thought.

"It's hard," she said after many long moments. "It's hard," she repeated ever so gently, *"I know."* I couldn't believe she said that. But as I looked up startled, I saw the truth of it in her wet eyes, and I knew then it was even hard for Joan. Her serenity was not a sign of hardness of heart, somehow acquired after years of practice—neither was her peaceful graciousness an absence of inner hurt—but simply a secure faith in a strength outside herself that allowed her to *bear bearably* what otherwise would have broken her in two. Quite simply she showed me her humanness—supported by the arms of Christ.

"You cry," she said, "and then you get up off your knees and wash your face and get on with it." Her natural way of being spiritual floored me. It was very typical of her. No stiff, stuffy sainthood here—I found instead a friendly friend and pilgrim true, who had been this way before—and lived to tell the tale.

"Just remember the priceless privilege we have of being married to these men of ours in the first place," she continued.

Telling me of the time she had received letters of commendation concerning her husband's war deeds and knelt to thank the Lord for saving his life, she said, "It was just as if I heard the Eternal say, 'But I didn't save him for you—I saved him for *Me!*'" That did it. We prayed and asked God to change my point of view, and keep on reminding me that He hadn't saved Stuart for *me,* but for *Him.*

I had sought to live up to my own high and noble expectations and fallen far, far short, failing to manipulate an attitude within myself of the model missionary manner. Then I had struggled to live up to Joan's expectations, and found in fact that my expectations of her expectations were completely false, and yet I had let those imaginary ideas produce so much needless misery. I walked home in the dark through the great beech trees that creaked with the might and importance of their age and found myself glorying in the biting wind. A few more steps and I would be home and safe from the cold, and that seemed exactly to fit my mood as I thought of the icy atmosphere of my self-inflicted pity parties. How thankful I was that I was leaving them behind for the warmth that waited for me in acceptance. Throwing back my head, I laughed up into the huge branches that reminded me of the outstretched everlasting arms I had been avoiding for so long.

"Oh, God," I shouted to the darkened sky, "I'm *coming home"*—and the moaning of the wind seemed to carry a soft, sweet echo of the Eternal's voice back to me saying—

"You should have come sooner."

"You're right," I answered softly—"of course. My husband's arms are on the other side of the Atlantic, my children's arms are too small to fit around my trouble, and my mother's arms are full of her own agonies. Joan used hers to point me to Yours—so where can I go but to heaven?"

"You should have come sooner," He said again, ever so gently.

"I should have indeed," I replied with a sigh—"I should have indeed!"

To Be a Friend: Application and Journal

....

1. Scripture says older women are to teach younger women, particularly about marriage (Titus 2:3–5). Read the passage. In which of these areas do you need guidance? Who do you know who may be able to come alongside you? Do you know a younger woman (perhaps a newlywed or mother of toddlers) who could use your friendship?

2. Do "servanthood" and "leadership" seem like contradictory terms? Why should a Christian leader get her hands dirty?

3. As you serve and interact with people, how self-conscious are you? Do you need to be more or less aware of yourself? Why?

4. Has the question of women's roles been troublesome for you? How have you begun to resolve it? What further steps can you take to understand this issue?

. . . .

For Action:
Read Proverbs 31. As you read, take notes. How does this picture
differ from our usual image of a godly woman?

. . . .

Chapter Seven

....

Peggy

....

*H*aving come to terms with loneliness and begun to use it as a positive force rather than a negative force, I discovered the hours would pass a lot more quickly if they were filled. Not that I needed to manufacture events to fill the void. We already had two little events called David and Judy who were busy doing *that!* The evenings were the problem. Seven in the evening saw the babes washed and bedded for the night, and then I would bank the coal fire high and settle down with some knitting or mending to while the hours away. Joan had told me that when she was busy all day and all night, she fell into bed at the end of a day too tired to suffer the insomniac's disease.

But I couldn't help feeling a little trapped and isolated stuck down at the main gateway, away from all that life and vigor up at the hall. It wasn't that there wasn't plenty of laboring to be done at home. It was just boredom with the household routines and a longing for some adult company. I realized I was in bad shape when Joan called down to the lodge and asked me to take the guest speaker to the train station. I was glad to comply. A fully grown human was like a species from another planet after having been shut up for a few rainy weeks with my two- and three-year-olds. To my horror, in the course of our ride, I found myself turning to him and telling him to "look at the little bunny rabbits playing in the pretty grass!" He gave me a somewhat startled look and told me I could stop throwing my arm in front of him every time we went around a corner as he was not sitting in a car chair.

Giggling over the recollection, I began another row of the cardigan I was making and decided to fill an evening with happy memories. That would surely make the hours go by. Stoking up the fire with more black, shiny coal, I thought about Middle Lodge—as our home was called.

It was a quaint home—hundreds of years old with walls about three feet thick. The problem was there wasn't much space left when they finished with the walls, and we experienced close fellowship. But it was *home* and we loved it. We never minded the cramped situation at all. We ate in a very small place I nicknamed "The Cozy" that could get pretty cold in wintertime. "You must have been thinking of its size rather than its temperature," my mother remarked wryly while visiting us one day. I noticed my son David was eating with his gloves on and nodded in bitter agreement.

The gatehouses that flanked the periphery of Capernwray's wooded land had been used to house working students, and our lodge had been no exception. Before our family arrived it had been home for lots of young stalwart Germans who had come to work for their keep at the conference center. As we began to move all our belongings into place, I heard a cheerful German song floating out from under the bathroom door. One student had been left behind. When he finally emerged, we all introduced ourselves. His name was Claus, and he was a carpenter by trade. We liked him a lot, which was just as well, as he informed Stuart that he had decided to stay on and live with us (before we really had an opportunity to invite him). Though we were somewhat taken aback wondering just where we could fit him in, we told him that would be fine.

A week later as he was taking another bath, a friend of ours decided to do us a good turn and fix the immersion heater that hung on the wall outside the bathroom. Suddenly his hand slipped and the screwdriver burrowed deep into the wires. Since he had omitted the elementary precaution of turning the electricity off, the friend was blown backward through the door! Claus abruptly stopped singing his song (we were sure we'd be singing one for Claus), but miraculously he was not hurt at all—although he suddenly decided to go and live up at the hall where he thought, no doubt, it would be safer.

Those were happy, happy days. Having two precious bundles of life to care for with only a few modern conveniences took its toll on my strength, but left me happy enough, except for some occasional fits of frustration during Stuart's long absences. At first I was tempted to turn to my mother to fill the void of loneliness, but then I remembered the words in the wedding service that talked of "leaving and cleaving," and I knew that Stuart's not being around did not negate the command.

Sitting by the side of that glowing fire with my two little ones safely tucked into bed, I began to think about that. I recalled an incident in Manchester just a few months after we were married and had moved into our new home. Stuart had settled into an easy chair to read the evening news. The athletes on the sports page leaped around the back of the newspaper, and those action-packed news items seemed to throw the stillness of my posture into sharp relief. The excitement of a new home and furniture, the fresh experience of buying and cooking for two, and getting used to the idea of being responsible for my side of the marriage had absorbed all my energies up to this point.

As I watched my new husband taking in world events, and as I rested momentarily from doing those totally unnecessary things a woman does when she is first married (like ironing the towels and the dust rags), I became aware of an unfamiliar lethargy, as if I was tiring of something. It was not a physical sensation at all, but something unidentifiable that was extremely disturbing. Sitting there watching Stuart, I thought about my day. Nothing out of the ordinary had happened, I thought. So many *new* things had been happening since we married, so maybe this sense of loss had to do with some *old* things that had ceased to happen.

It couldn't be that I was tired of the routine after only a few months, and yet I really did feel like I needed a change. But a change of what? I felt like a child tiring of playing with her dollhouse, wanting to play another game. But this was marriage, not some childish recreation I could opt out of. No wonder I found myself sitting so still. Guilt washed over me like turbulent ocean breakers, tumbling me around in disorienting foam. The newspaper walls growing out of my man's shoes and trousers built a barrier that shut me away from all that was familiar. I felt disconnected from reality. Suddenly and uncontrollably, big tears washed down my face. *What on earth is the matter?* I frantically questioned, hoping the stocks and shares would prove interesting enough distraction to Stuart to give me time to dry up. It wasn't that I wasn't in love; I was. It wasn't that I didn't have everything I wanted or needed; I did—or did I? There was definitely something irrevocably missing. What was it?—if it was indeed an *it* that wasn't there—or was it perhaps a *she?* There it was, I knew—Peggy! My own beloved mother. It took only the sound of her name in my heart and it was all over—the silent stream became a torrent. Down came the newspaper wall, and two concerned, but *very* practical eyes sized up the damp situation.

"What's the matter?" they inquired.

"I want my mother," I answered in pauses through the roar of the waterfall. Yes, I did—I wanted my mother. After five months? Yes, after five months. It's so ridiculous, and it was also so strange because I really didn't want her to be there in the same room with us. It was then I recognized that I was grieving. Grieving over the irrevocable chasm that marriage had put between my mother and me. "Leave and cleave," said the words in the marriage service—till death us do part. But where did cleaving leave my other relationships?

Maybe I shouldn't have gotten married so soon, I thought. *Perhaps I wasn't mature enough to handle the leaving bit yet.* As Stuart sympathetically lent me his big handkerchief (and then went back to his stocks and shares), I wondered if anyone else in the whole world had ever wanted her mother so soon after she was married like I did. I couldn't imagine that this was so—but even if somebody else had, that didn't help me. I questioned if my psychological umbilical cord had ever been severed, and if not, what it was going to take to do it. How could a few words whispered tremulously in front of witnesses and before the altar expect to rend asunder that bond of mother-daughter love? Stuart patiently emerged from his newspaper a second time to explain to me it wasn't the love that had to go—just the dependence—and that helped a bit.

But until then I hadn't thought of myself as being dependent on my mother. The truth was slowly coming home to me that I still was, and in this new relationship with Stuart I was supposed to have transferred my dependence. In other words, I had no more right to look first to my mother for that sense of safe authority-security.

My mind went back farther to the few weeks Stuart and I had lived with my parents immediately after we were married. Our home was beautiful and Stuart was thoroughly enjoying the luxury, good meals, and excellent, loving care he was getting from my mother. The only fly in the ointment was a cute, sleek black spaniel puppy who loved to bite his stockinged toes as he cleaned his shoes and jigged from one foot to the other. That he could put up with when everything else was so good. But *I* wanted to look after him. It wasn't the same baking a bit of the meal for the evening and showing him which was mine—I wanted to do it all. Actually I never needed to explain which bit was mine—*most of us already knew!* If I wasn't burning everyone's tongues with my red-hot jam—roly-poly, "like molten lead" my poor red-faced husband spluttered—then I was making lame excuses for the soufflé that looked like a pancake. It was no wonder the poor man didn't want to be left at my mercy.

But I was determined we get out on our own and off my parents' backs, and so one day in the middle of a terrible Liverpool smog (having just recovered from a severe dose of the flu) we piled everything into our little car and took off in the general direction of Manchester, our house, and our brand-new stove, the sole occupant. It had taken us a few months to laugh our way through first-time wallpapering antics and buy the essential furniture, and then the previous incident had occurred and I had found myself busy playing house all on my own—without my mother and wishing we were back with her. I remembered there had been nothing left for it but to sigh wetly and iron the towels all over again.

Sitting by the lodge fire all these years later, knitting that warm garment for my child, I chuckled softly, thanking God for a mother who had been able to let me go—in love.

Peggy had been the first to know when we were expecting our first baby. Her beautiful dark brown eyes had lit up with joy and excitement, and she immediately began making her own preparations for the event. Just as my mother had asked us to call her Peggy from our early child-hood days, perhaps anticipating the day she would lay aside her mother role for friendship's garments, so she told me now that she wanted to be called "Nanna" instead of grandmother, a name that apparently con-jured up in her mind too austere a picture and not the friend she was de-termined to be to our children, even as she had been to us.

We decided I would come home to Liverpool to have the baby so that Peggy could help us for a while. I will never forget bringing David home. Why weren't the bands out, the flags flying, and the cannons fir-ing? Did ever a human being feel so much inordinate pride of achieve-ment before? Well—looking at Stuart's shining face—maybe one.

We tiptoed inside the big hallway and Peggy met us, cooing in typically grandmotherish delight toward the bundle in my arms, which was wrapped in fabric, moving gently. She told me my old room was ready, and then she turned and went into the kitchen to busy herself with lunch. I remember repressing a great desire to shout, "Come back, don't leave me. You've done this before." But I knew her casual gesture and careful exit had been her strong reminder that I was now a mother too, and no one in the whole world could be account-able for this priceless bundle of life but my husband and me.

I went upstairs to my old room, pink and white just as it had al-ways been. There in the wall was the book niche that had contained God's Book commanding me to reach out and touch it all those years ago. And now I stood there with my own child in my arms, totally awed by my responsibility. Stuart had stayed downstairs, and I was left watching David stir and stretch and shape his little rubber mouth into a noise for food. There were no nurses in my little pink and white room, no doctors, friends, husband, mother, or sister. Just David and I. I thought suddenly of a prayer that Peggy had told me she prayed every day of her life. It was very simple and, I would have to say, it had been answered very thoroughly. It said—"Oh God, make me a good mother." I knelt by that bed and I prayed it too—adding, "like Peggy."

After attending to our babe's urgent needs and somehow managing to change him all by myself, I carried him downstairs triumphantly and presented him in the kitchen—meeting Peggy's proud, proud eyes, which seemed to say, "Well done, you did it on your own. You'll be all right, and so will David—you'll see, however inadequate you feel."

How do mothers get all that wisdom? I murmured, as the lodge fire died down and my thoughts were interrupted by the cry of a child upstairs. Cuddled inside a red tartan rug that shut us in to each other, I rocked Judy asleep, pondering if, when the time came, I would be a good enough mother to be able to let go. As I rocked that little bundle of girl who needed me so, it seemed almost impossible to comprehend. *What would happen,* I wondered, *when I wasn't needed anymore?* How would I cope with that? Looking at my babe's so sweet and passive face, I prayed that the Lord would help me do for her what had been done for me, and never allow me to become so possessive that I would thereby destroy the very love I sought to keep. "Leave and cleave," I murmured to Judy's sleeping form. You have to leave and cleave—that's what marriage is all about.

Most weekends in the summer while we were living at Capernwray, Father traveled up to the Lake District with friends to fish for salmon. Sometimes he brought Mother and left her with me for the day. I would get up early and bake things I knew she would like—shortbread, scones, and trifle. Why I did I'll never know, because she never ate more than half of one—"Just to sample them," she'd say. In fact she used to appear at the kitchen door with a truckload of food for us, and at lunch time she would bring out a brown paper bag containing her lunch: a banana she had brought to save us having to feed her.

She would ask most apologetically if I could furnish her with a piece of bread to go with it. After a while I came to understand her need to give and the joy this brought to her. I tried to accept all her generosity with grace, trusting she saw how much I appreciated it all.

How I used to look forward to those special visits. After all, no one outside the family was really interested in the appearance of baby's first teeth, or the expanding of little David's capacity to master new areas of math, or the wonder of the words "Hasn't he grown" to a parent's proud ears. But Peggy didn't just come to *say* things—she came to *do* things as well. What she said was usually matched by what she did, and as she'd never been afraid of hard work—not even a lodge full of it—she'd have a cup of tea with me and then "get cracking."

As we chattered together, we would laugh all day as Peggy set the pace and made the humor, constantly poking fun at herself. She had somehow nurtured an ability to stand back and watch a rerun of a situation, determined to be amused by her own reaction or laugh into subjection any weakness that she saw. We busied ourselves with diapers and cleaning and cooking and bed making, keeping up an endless repartee of recollections—all of which were brushed with hilarious afterthoughts, usually at Peggy's expense.

She reminded me of the time we were vacationing for the summer months on a houseboat on Lake Windemere. Father joined us on the weekends, but in between times Peggy was game to be captain, scullery maid, head cook, and bottle washer—and holiday maker par excellence for us children. There were a few things, however, she was not such an expert at, like battening down in a storm, or trusting us to tie the dinghy safely up before we all went to bed at night. She was the first to giggle at the memory of the night she threaded the rope through her porthole when we were all asleep and tied it around her wrist, saying in effect, "Take my boat, take me!" How we laughed as we reminisced about that one.

One of the most basic lessons I learned from my mother was her sense of openness and honesty. She could never bear to harbor anything and had to "have it out" as soon as possible. She always had to tell us what was on her mind and clear the air. My sister practiced a similar philosophy, saying, "Life's too short to fall out—I won't do it!" But for me, it was harder. Telling half the truth, resorting to a little white lie, or taking an "anything for peace" stance never seemed to do me any harm, but whenever she could, Peggy pushed me into being truthful in my statements and actions. She encouraged me to put things right with people immediately. I'm sure it was this healthy training that helped me later to keep things right in my relationship with God and thus keep the lines open to heaven.

One day when I was about fourteen, Father had made a roaring fire in our cozy lounge. He was listening to his favorite composer, and I was sprawled on the floor reading *Hiawatha*. Mother was working in the kitchen as usual, preparing a lovely meal for the family. Father glanced up from his fishing magazine and quietly ordered me to go and help her. I was mad, but enough in awe of him that I didn't dare answer back. Resorting to a sullen, silent selfishness, I stormed into the kitchen and arrived at Mother's side like a young tornado ready to blow the vegetables apart.

"What do you want?" she asked.

"Dad sent me to help," I muttered menacingly.

"Well, with a face like that I can do without it," she replied. "Off with you!"

Knowing what Father would say, I hurriedly changed my tune, begging her to let me stay. But allowing me to know in no uncertain terms how she felt and rebuking me for my attitude, she sent me packing. But where could I go? Certainly not back into the lounge. In the no-man's land of the ice-cold hall, I hopped from one foot to the other, looking first at the closed kitchen door and then at the closed lounge door. Finally, deciding that Father would think I'd done my bit and was through, I whistled my way back to my book. Therein lay my deceitfulness. I just couldn't walk in and tell him what I'd done—instead I laid a lie on top of my teenage temper tantrum and tried to bluff it out.

It took the Lord Jesus Christ to change me and begin to help me tell my feelings and failings openly and honestly with people. Tucking

Judy safely under the covers in that little English lodge, I sang her a lullaby. Judy smiled as she slumbered—or it may well have been a grimace, I couldn't be sure. (I had an awful voice.) I decided to decide it was a smile and knew I could return to the fireside.

Peggy would be glad to see the two little ones slumbering so happily. She always tried to see that her children slept at peace with the world. I thought of the times I had gone to bed disturbed by some boy problem or other, and how even in those turbulent teenage years she had sought to send me to bed in peace.

I remembered her slight bewilderment as she faced an extremely intense but very nice Christian young man who had come to visit me after I had been sick. I had returned from college and was teaching in Liverpool at the time. I don't think Mother had been too impressed with the few boys I had brought home since my conversion, and I could hardly blame her as some of them were a little strange. This one looked fine, and what was more he carried a huge box of chocolates for the invalid. Well, now he must be partway normal, Mother reckoned.

"How is Jill?" he asked politely.

"Oh, she's practically better, thank you," answered Peggy, ushering him into the living room and stretching out her hands, offering to accept the chocolates for me. His face fell.

Clutching the candies, he said, "Oh well, if she's better, I'll keep these then—I wouldn't want to waste the Lord's money." Leaving my mother speechless, he and the chocolates disappeared.

The same young man later told me that God had instructed him to marry me. I didn't want to be his wife one little bit—but he had been a committed believer so much longer than I had that I thought God might be trying to tell me something. I couldn't sleep; hearing my sobs, Peggy perched on my bed and gently inquired the nature of my trouble. I burbled out the story, and she disarmed me within minutes saying, "Oh, Jill, as if God would ask you to marry someone you didn't love!" And then she went on to tell me the story of the chocolates. We both ended up giggling like a couple of schoolgirls—and I eventually went to sleep happy, for Peggy believed in that.

Peggy

* * *

Thinking of Peggy's shyness—the sweet, tender, terrible shyness that had chased her behind her mother's skirts as a child and had made her want to disappear when someone called her name—I marveled at her courage in facing Shirley and me with some basic facts when she saw us making bad choices or obvious mistakes. She always respected our privacy and "trusted us twice"—an essential skill that mothers should cultivate. To trust once requires not much more than most can give, but to trust again when trust has been abused requires another quality of confidence altogether. That needs a belief in the child, a determination to think the best, and a confidence in God's intervention when everyone believes the worst. I knew *for that quality I would need the power of God.*

The fire had gone out, my dreaming was ended, and it was time to go to bed. As I went up the winding stairs that night, I had the strangest foreboding that Mother was in trouble, but I pushed it away thinking it was only because I had spent the evening in rememberings. It was Mother, not I, I reminded myself, who possessed that sixth sense when something was wrong with one of the family. The next time I saw her she told me Daddy was sick. My father had been struggling with cancer, so I knew she meant something serious. I never asked her for the details and she didn't offer the information. She just told me the doctors couldn't do anything else, and she asked me to pray that she would be able to make him as happy as possible to the end. How someone with cancer could be happy to the end, I didn't know, but I watched my mother make it as possible as it could be. When it was over and Father had become the first of our family to go to heaven, I sent Peggy a little poem that I found. It said—

> *Better to be like a lark on high*
> *Singing for joy 'gainst a cloudless sky*
> *Better to know no sorrow or pain*
> *No darkness or death,*
> *But to live again.*

> *Better to breathe in Heaven's pure air*
> *A lamb that is safe in the Shepherd's care*
> *Better far better with Christ to be*
> *Living and loved through eternity.*
> —R. E. Cleeve, *Vision Card #173*

I didn't know how to comfort a person who had been severed in two, but I knew Someone who could—and I committed my beloved mother to Him who promised me "A bruised reed shall he not break"—and asked Him to mend her heart.

A little before my father died our third child was born, and my hours were filled with the demands of that new life and the refereeing of David and Judy's time together. My day started terribly early. Before I had three children I had given a talk to a ladies' group on daily devotions, but it now lay buried at the bottom of a drawer. I had to admit that *daily commotions* had taken their place. I just couldn't wake up before the first baby's cry, and once the bedlam started, just where in our small lodge could I ever find a quiet place to meet with God? Three pairs of small hands clutched at me all day long. If they weren't clutching at me, they were clutching at each other, and I'd have to de-clutch them and watch and see that the baby didn't get trodden underfoot in the confined space.

One morning I ignored baby Peter's screams and went ahead and read my Bible anyway. I could hear David and Judy happily playing some game and therefore reckoned Pete's cries were an "I want to play too" tantrum. After the wailing music had continued for some time, I thought I'd better investigate and went through to their bedroom. The bunk beds stood against the walls and there was a bar across the top to prevent anyone from falling out. From it dangled Peter, who had been hooked up there to keep him out of the way. When I lifted him down, his little arms remained stretched straight above his head, and I had to massage them back to life again.

Well, now, I reasoned, if I couldn't meet the Eternal before the day began, then I'd better meet Him when it was over. But when it was over so was I, and I decided it wasn't very polite to give God the most worn-out part of me. What was I to do? Looking around the living room the next day my eye fell on the playpen that just about filled the room. That would do it! I clambered in and put the children *out* and found a place at last where I was all alone, but I still had a vantage point from which I could keep an eye on the children. The little imps rattled the bars in fury trying to get at me—in fact, that was the only time I could remember them wanting to get *in* instead of *out*. I told them they would just have to wait, as it was Mummy's turn in the playpen. What a difference those few brief moments with God's Law began to make.

I couldn't imagine how young mothers like me with a crop of young children could ever cope without the wise words and encouragement of that Book. To begin with, I had awful fears. Some were valid I'm sure, but many were not. Some were nightmarish flashes of horror that I really needed help with. At that point in my life all of them had to do with my children. I feared that I would wake up in the morning and find the newborn baby dead in his crib, or that the toddler would choke on his food. Then sometimes I had a gruesome "daymare" about one of them being put in the washing machine by an imaginary torturer who then forced me to switch on the machine. Other more ghastly ideas flooded into my fertile imagination, and I'd turn to God and cry for help; it would always, always be found.

"God hath not given us the spirit of fear," said the apostle Paul, "but of power, and of love, and of a sound mind" (2 Timothy 1:7). I had worried at such times if I was indeed losing my senses. That particular word spoke strongly to me, telling me the gifts of God were not those things at all, and if the Eternal was not giving me the spirit of fear, I had no need to take gifts from the devil. God had given me a sound mind, and I needed to bring each wild notion along to Him to deal with. Practicing thought control was not a new concept to me, but bringing my delinquent thoughts under Christ's control was a new and relieving experience indeed. In other words, what I could not control He could, and if I asked Him to—He would.

Growing in confidence, I began to dare to enjoy my children and stop expecting the most catastrophic things to happen to them daily. When I took the babies to the local clinic to weigh them and swap baby talk with other young mothers, other women told their similar fears. I would listen and then be able to tell them that I too experienced such forebodings, but then I always added, *"For that I need the peace of God."* One by one these young mothers began to ask what I meant, and I explained motherhood was God's brainchild. Seeing He had the original notion, He had some more good ideas how it worked, and if they could only get on the wavelength, He'd let them in on the secrets. Some believed, and some decided to go it alone without Him. I couldn't imagine how they would cope, or how their children would manage without a meaningful knowledge of God, but that was their choice. I was only responsible for my commitment, not theirs, and all I needed to know and sometimes to testify to was simply this thing— *"For this I need the presence of God."*

I determined to be the optimist I wasn't by nature. When I walked into the living room and found Judy neatly parceled up, completely covered in the blanket upon which she had been lying, and found that David had done it, I gradually learned not to suspect I had a potential murderer on my hands, but just to say, "I'm so glad you're such a tidy little fellow, David, but *please* don't wrap Judy up every time you find her lying on a blanket." When Judy sucked her thumb I asked for release from my guilt trips wondering what "mother-lack" had caused it.

"Have you hugged your child today?" the bumper sticker accused me. *How many hugs are enough?* I wondered frantically. Who's to know and who's to tell the poor mother of young children when to stop or how hard to hug? I thought on down the years in horror, wondering if I would spend my life tortured by the worry of not knowing the answers to that apparently most important question. And what about when they were teenagers and I couldn't hug them anymore? A dark thought grinned at me from my imaginary future, and I saw in my mind's eye another bumper sticker that would frighten the living daylights out of me. It would say, "Who *else* has hugged your child today?" No, these sorts of imaginings were no good—for me or for my little ones. I must remember, if it depended on my doing my best— poor children. But it didn't. As far as I was concerned, the Eternal had promised to care for and keep them. I could trust Him also to help me live free from whipping myself for all their mistakes.

"I had a child and put him in paradise," God reminded me through His Word, "and he still went wrong. Was that My fault, do you think? Bring them up as well as you know how in the nurture and admonition of the Lord and commit them to Me—remembering you must always reckon on their gift of free will playing a part. They too must make their own choice to go *My* way, and so it's not always your fault when it doesn't work out quite as you hoped and dreamed."

What marvelous trust God placed in us, I thought in awe. *And what a risk He took!* Fancy allowing us the chance to build eternal values into our children's lives, telling us, "Train up a child in the way he should go," promising us then that "when he is old, he will not depart from it." God had given us the ability as parents to guide our own, and as far as Stuart and I were concerned, that meant guiding them into the way of Jesus. I realized it was this dimension that made a Christian mother different from just a mother. She had the grand ability to know God and make Him known to her child.

Yes, I could teach our children the Eternal's ways, I thought excitedly. That would fill the lonely hours while Stuart was traveling. Then another thought occurred to me. The verse could have ended: "Train up a child in the way he should go—and walk there yourself once in a while." There has to be the training of example to go along with it, I mused. The do-as-I-do that I had seen in Peggy's life and that I could seek to emulate, and not just the do-as-I-say bit.

But there was one more way that verse could have ended: "Train up a child in the way he should go—and he will train up the parent in the way *he* should go." I was beginning to learn so much from my children and knew with an excited anticipation we had only just begun. "I guess that's why we parents usually need to start off so young," I commented to God.

I think He smiled.

To Be a Friend:
Application and Journal

· ·

1. When are you and your mother on the best terms? What do you enjoy most about your relationship at those times? If she is no longer alive, what brings the fondest memories?

2. What is the most common cause for conflict with your mother? How do you usually respond at those times—do you like that response?

3. In what areas has your mother released you into adulthood? When does she still treat you like a youngster?

4. On what occasions has your mother shown pride in your achievements? What skills has she appreciated? If she has never expressed such pride, list three times she should have done so.

Chapter Eight

Angela

$\mathcal{S}$tuart's brother Bernard and his wife Helen lived in the city of Manchester, which was about an hour and a half's journey from us. One day we received a letter from Helen about an old school friend of hers who she thought might be helped by coming to spend a few days with us at Capernwray. She told us her story. Her name was Angela and she worked as a stewardess for a British airline. Billy Graham had been invited by various churches in Manchester to hold some special meetings in the huge soccer stadium, and Angela's boyfriend suggested they go hear him. The campaign had been attacked by the press and the whole operation labeled as an "emotional carnival." Some church leaders had looked down their ecclesiastical noses in disdain and wondered aloud (in the hearing of the press) how this American evangelist dared to think *we British* needed his help in the first place.

As it turned out, the unfavorable coverage did the Crusade a good turn. The British sense of fair play came to the rescue, and the public decided the underdog (in this case Billy Graham) needed at least to be given a chance to defend himself. Accordingly, many of the city residents, including Angela, decided to go to the Crusade and judge for themselves.

There was nothing highly emotional about sitting in the cool

Manchester air in that vast stadium surrounded by families with wiggling, distracting children, she had thought. In fact she wondered to herself how she was going to be able to concentrate at all when the time came to listen to the sermon. She was also curious to see what happened at the conclusion of the service, having heard that people were swept along by something akin to hysteria and went out to make some sort of fools of themselves. As soon as the message began, however, she forgot everything else and found herself riveted to her seat, gripped by the words she was hearing. Christianity had been presented not as a panacea for all ills, not as something that would necessarily make a person feel good inside, but rather as *the truth*. People were being urged to consider the claims of Christ not only so they could be better people, or so that those who were lame and needed a crutch could walk, but simply because Christ was divine and therefore had a valid claim on their lives.

The whole thing sounded profound yet practical, and somehow as right as anything had ever sounded to Angela's ears. Hardly able to believe herself, she accepted the evangelist's invitation to inquire further, and rising from her seat she walked forward that she might find out how to know the Eternal personally.

"Hmm, this sounds like a *'Jesus Connection,'*" I murmured, as I finished reading Helen's letter, wondering if we were to be part of it all.

Sure enough, Angela accepted our invitation. We welcomed her into the family, found her a cubbyhole to sleep in, and set about getting to know her. "I don't think I want to continue working for the airlines," she confided after a few days. "I'd love to be on staff at a place like this!" I tried to think of some way an air stewardess could fit into the mission, and I had a colorful vision of this smart, attractive blue-eyed girl with her most attractive personality, dressed in her snazzy uniform, instructing everyone in Ben Hur's Chariot to fasten their seat belts as they *took off* from the train station to the hall. Little did I know that the Father was masterminding it all into place.

Stuart's secretary, Cathy, had felt for some time she would like to work in France. She was fluent in the language, loved the French people, had a great aptitude for accounting, and had a particular caring spirit for the underprivileged. She also had come from a Roman Catholic background. For more than a year she had been asking God to show her if this was all her bright idea or His plan. But part of her problem was she had no idea where to go or where she would fit in. She wondered just how she was to start and find the right niche for her particular talents and gifts.

The very week Angela came to stay with us we had a missionary speaker at the hall. Seeing it was the first time he had spoken to the students, Cathy was curious to hear what he had to say and went along with us to listen. She could hardly believe her ears as he began to give a report about his work among the underprivileged in the French city of Lille.

After the meeting, over a cup of coffee, the missionary told some of his concerns to Stuart. "The work is just beginning," he told my husband, "but already I am inundated with names of people who need visiting. We are living in a depressed area, the poverty is unbelievable, and now I find I need a secretary. I am looking for someone who can handle the finances of the mission, is fluent in French, and has a sensitive understanding of the Roman Catholic Church. We also want to begin a youth program like the one you have here, so we need someone who can handle that as well." The Eternal smiled and so did Stuart as he guided the missionary out of the office saying, "Let me introduce you to her; her name is Cathy and she has been waiting for you." It was undoubtedly the *Connection* again.

What excitement we felt as later that night Stuart told the story to Angie and me, saying when he'd finished, "We are going to miss Cathy, and I'm wondering who is going to interpret the messages for all our French young people in the summer conferences. She has been such an excellent translator." The Eternal smiled again, for His replacement was busy eating toast and honey and drinking our tea, wondering in awe how all this could be. *God's clocks keep perfect time,* she was thinking, *for these new friends of mine have no way of knowing that I have already written my resignation.* We certainly had no way of guessing how her heart was beginning to beat louder and louder in anticipation of the words she was about to blurt out. Before she could say anything, however, I playfully poked her in the ribs and said, "It's a pity you are an air stewardess and not a secretary, Angie."

"I am a trained secretary," she answered quietly.

"Well, it's a pity you don't speak French then," I teased.

"I do," she answered more softly still. "I spent a whole year at a French university."

And so Angela went home to collect her clothes, finish her airline responsibilities, and tell her surprised family she was going to be Stuart Briscoe's secretary and, she suspected, his wife's best friend.

In the days that followed, as Angie and I began to know each other more thoroughly, I remembered that Joan had cautioned me against having a close personal relationship with anyone on staff. "Leaders can't usually afford such luxuries," she had explained. "In a close community such as ours, friendships that become too exclusive just cause jealousy and problems all around." I had listened with respect, but as Stuart's duties called him away and I found myself more and more alone, I knew I needed someone of like mind to relate to and discuss the joys and sorrows of my growing responsibilities. With Angie I found a friendship of equals that was something quite new to me.

Up to this time I had been in the position either of needing help from someone a little ahead of me in the Christian life, or else giving advice to someone who had not been on the way quite as long as I had. But Angie had grown so quickly in her love and knowledge of God that I soon found a freedom of friendship I had not enjoyed before. It was such a relief not to have to be a blessing on the one hand, and not to have to be learning a lesson on the other. What a relief to be able to relax and enjoy another person for her own sake! Angie and I did enjoy each other. She could always see the funny side of life, taking completely ordinary events, and, with no trouble at all, caricaturing them into the hilarious. Being an inveterate mimic she would produce a one-man pantomime at Christmas, taking off one staff member after another, picking up our mannerisms and forcing us to laugh at ourselves, however unflatteringly portrayed. But it was Angie's musical abilities and particularly her expertise with the guitar that linked her up with the *Connection* that had begun to be laid around our neighborhood.

As David and Judy's circle of friends got bigger, I decided to get to know the little people that they brought home to play with. I gathered a whole bunch of playful toddlers together in the living room, plonked Judy's carry cot down in the middle of them, and started a Sunday school. It was somewhat informal and very much fun. I seemed to hear Janet's encouraging words from the past telling me to start where I was with what I had. I was about to be reminded all over again that guidance from God is not a question of a blinding light from heaven, or a "Big Brother" type voice from among the stars, but usually *the most obvious thing to do or the opportunity right under your nose.* I needed to be alerted to the fact that the daily *Connection* was probably disguised as a four-year-old climbing a tree, an old lady rocking in her chair, the barber cutting and snipping away, or even the grocery boy who helped me carry my parcels.

As the little group of children in our Sunday school began to multiply, we looked around for a bigger space to accommodate them all. Angie felt we should invite their parents along so that they could sit in on the class and see what we were teaching their children. To our surprise many of them came and sat all crunched up on top of each other and not a little embarrassed, I'm sure, as we *were* rather confined.

Angie played her guitar and the children sang their songs, I told the Bible story, and then it was time to pray. Pudgy hands pressed hotly together readied themselves for that holy exercise. Zippered eyes flickered with the strain of staying closed. Some peeped furtively through silky lashes at their mummies' faces. "Let's start with 'thank you' prayers," I suggested. A few prayed their own sentence prayers, and then on we went to the "please" ones. There was no problem with knowing what to say here; in fact, the flood of words was difficult to stop. It was the "sorry" prayers that they had trouble with (like all of us). After a heavy silence broken only by a little boy asking God to forgive his sister for giving him a hard time, I hastily closed the session and announced it was time to go home. As the parents shook hands with us at the door, one lady who had been pressed by the sheer volume of bodies into a **V**-shape in the corner of the room invited us to come and use her big farmhouse kitchen next time.

Angie and I smiled excitedly, sensing a *Connection,* and were to be proved right. Week after week, in that lady's beautiful old kitchen amid the steamy smell of caldrons of homemade soup, the children brought their friends to learn of Jesus. Angie loved them all. Down on the floor she would go to sit cross-legged among them, leveling her love to their height and caring most deeply for their needs.

From that time on the Father began to mold Angie and me into a team and give us dual assignments. I realized early on in our relationship that only in Christ could women be so safely close as we. His authority guarded our affection, keeping it sweet, and preventing it from crossing lines that would make it unhealthy in any degree. Our mutual dependence on Him enabled us to enjoy the best, forgive the worst, and, most important of all, allow each other the freedom to develop other friendships.

To be honest, there were times when the introduction of a third party who sought to make a close friend of one or the other of us resulted in an uneasy tussle of emotion for me. I found myself on not a few occasions behaving like an overgrown schoolgirl, guarding the territory of our relationship with a silly childish possessiveness that insisted on competing for Angie's attention or trying to buy her approval in some way or other. I would realize I was manipulating situations and even neglecting other duties, simply to prevent my rival from spending time with my friend. Then I knew it was time to talk to God concerning the matter. There was always somewhere to go with it of course, and in the still point the Eternal encouraged me to verbalize my jealousy, offering to exchange it for His giving and His yielding love. Then the sullen "green" monster would lose his grip, and our relationship would be free of clutching, damaging selfishness again.

Interest in the Bible and what it had to say began to gather momentum in the neighborhood. It was such a help to find Angie willing to have a go at any need that cropped up. She didn't have to be up front giving the orders, but if she needed to be, she would do it and do it well. It takes a lot of character to play in *second place* when you have the *first place* gifts, but that was no problem to Angie as she possessed all the character necessary. "It matters more than tongue can tell/to play the second fiddle well" says the couplet. Anyway, as far as she was concerned, second was first if God was asking her to do it. But there was another reason Angie decided to make playing the second fiddle matter. She had an inkling she might well be conducting the whole orchestra one day, and if that were indeed to be the case she reckoned she had better stay as close as she could to the action and learn by my mistakes.

The time had come for me to see if I could get along with my best friend in a working relationship. Struggling with the awkwardness of it, I decided that if the situation had to do with the ministry I would just *tell* her what to do—but if it was outside those boundaries I would *ask* her. It took a lot of nerve for her to face me with her complaint and say, "Jill, I like to be *asked,* not *told,* you know." How thankful I am she helped me see that there is *no* place for rudeness or bossiness in the family of God.

She didn't just do the things I was asking her to do, either. If Angie saw a need, she didn't sit back and say in an important sort of voice, "Something has to be done." She got up and did it. Like getting involved with *the Beasties*—her affectionate term for the younger brothers and sisters of the teenagers we had been reaching from the nearby town. Nine- to twelve-year-olds roamed in packs, creating havoc. They were unrestrained, uncontrollable, and unloved in the mass. Most church groups had decided to wait till these kids were fifteen before trying to reach them (or in jail—so they wouldn't have to bother). But Angie caught the Major's vision for such scalawags when he said, "Boys will be boys, but one day boys will be men!"

Pulling on her blue jeans and grabbing her windbreaker, her short, thick hair cut cleverly in casual carefreeness that was ideal for a hike in the woods or a chase up the mountains, her blue eyes twinkling in a sweet warmth of appreciation of a junior high kid's confusion, Angie challenged *the Beasties* to take her on. They accepted. "You mean you're going to start a club just for us?" they gasped.

"You bet," she answered, and every spare minute of her time from that moment was spent in such exciting pursuits as building bonfires or trying to put them out, refereeing the soccer game, or setting off the alarm for the rescue squad when she inadvertently lost one of the boys in a quarry after a great game of cops and robbers. Soon the kids were far too busy to get into trouble any more, but if they did they knew Angie would stick with them in it and through it.

Her deep love for God was transmitted during those outings, and at the conclusion of such adventures, often wet and disheveled, she would flop into a kitchen chair telling me with soft wonder about the talk she'd had with Andy as they spun stones across the river, or the prayer she'd prayed with Geoff about his drunken dad while waiting for the sausages to sizzle. "You've got to give them time and yourself," she'd murmur, "not classroom rote. *They're going to open up when they're ready, not when we are, so we'd better be around!*" Recruiting older kids to *be around* them too, we were reminded that giving teenagers responsibility before they were ready for it produced the very maturity they looked as though they'd never have.

Every so often Angie would try to throw some sort of cultural event into the scheme of things, endeavoring to add a bit of class to their lives. One day she decided to pile them into the club van and take them off to a sleepy and picturesque village to visit a lovely old church. On weekdays in the country districts, the buildings were never locked up, and so, having the sense I hadn't had years earlier, she took them on their historical outing when the church was otherwise empty. All went well for at least four reverent minutes, and she was feeling very proud of their subdued behavior, when suddenly the historical became hysterical. The sound of rolling thunder caused her to spin around with a dread sense of foreboding. Down that ancient aisle shot the trolley used for the funeral caskets, and riding high on top perched a triumphant "Beastie" propelled at a terrible rate by another two. It was time to forget the culture and leave.

* * *

Three years after starting to work with those "mini-club" projects, Angie commented to me that practically all the children she had started with were still with us. "I bet we'd only have reached a third of them now if we hadn't started when we did," she said.

"Well then, why don't we take it one step further," I suggested. "Let's use the ones you know best and start children's groups in the schools using *them* as mini-leaders."

It was the *Connection* again. Nearly every one of them had younger brothers and sisters, and all of them went to school locally. Angie sold the idea to her club. They got busy producing and duplicating invitations, taking them to their own school gates and handing them out. Fifteen-year-old Madelain begged the use of her parents' garage for a clubhouse, and in no time at all had filled it.

Now it was time to train the leaders to train the children, and as time went on, time to train the leaders to train the leaders. The philosophy was very simple: pass on what you know to someone else who doesn't know it, who is willing to pass it on to the next person. The Law of the Eternal nodded its head, saying, "The things that thou hast heard . . . commit thou to faithful men, who shall be able to teach others also" (2 Timothy 2:2). The key to it was right there—find the faithful. Not necessarily the trained, clever, or gifted. It didn't even say the old or the successful. It was *the faithful* who would be committed to the things we committed to them. This way the *Connection* should continue ad infinitum.

Our common caring for the good of the many young people who were now involved knit Angie and me together in a deeply enriching way. Life was profitable and purposeful, and I had much to share on the blue airmail forms that spun happily across the Atlantic Ocean to my husband in the States. It was amazing how the ministry had spread, I thought, when I remembered it had all begun with a handful of toddlers in our living room.

The *Connections* connected. Bobby had a granny who wanted to know if we had a class for senior citizens. We didn't until he asked us.

Soon Granny invited her friends, who invited theirs, and a few months later there were more than forty grannies who'd brought along their daughters, all meeting together in the little stone chapel on Capernwray's grounds. One day I invited a friend of ours to come and speak to them. He was a local farmer, and he brought some eggs and baby chicks with him by way of illustration. Starting off in grand style, having the women from that farming community in rapt attention, he was suddenly interrupted by an old woman leaning over to her neighbor and inquiring in the habit of the hard of hearing who are loud of speaking, "Are them ducks or goslings?" Our farmer friend invited us to tour his chicken farm and receive some elementary instruction in such matters as the difference between ducks and geese.

While we were there, we were introduced to Anette, a farmer's wife who lived nearby. She was sweet and shy and just needed connecting. As soon as she stepped into the still point, she reached out her hand and pulled her husband right in there beside her. Norman and Anette had a good marriage already, but once the Eternal took over they discovered the excitement of handing all their possessions over to Him to do with as He pleased. "We've been wanting to help you with the teenagers," they told us quietly one day, "but we are stuck out here in the middle of nowhere and have our little ones to care for and no one to baby-sit for us—so we don't know how this could be worked out." The Father smiled, for He knew we were about to overflow the small upper room we'd been hiring in the village and that it was time for the kids to establish a headquarters of their own.

Next to Norman and Anette's small country cottage there sat a barn. The Eternal, having used such a place once two thousand years ago, was about to make use of one again. And so use of that modern stable was given, and we began to set up house, whitewashing the old stone walls—not to mention whitewashing each other, which was great fun. Competent teenage hands knocked wood into bench and table shapes. Matting spread the floor to catch the Cokes and crisps that soon would drip from jumping, bumping bodies, happily making themselves at home. The doing of the project was invaluable, bringing us all together with a common objective.

Once in and ready to go, we set about organizing the various activities that had been started spontaneously. We discovered all sorts of exciting things that had been going on that we knew absolutely nothing about. How thrilling that in the loose-knit fellowship of which we were all a part, there was an easy and compliant acknowledgment of our authority, and yet each one knew he had his own direct access to the Father. Many of the kids had been busy asking Him to help them make their own unique *Connection.*

Some of the boys had started a soccer team and joined a local league. They would pray before the kickoff (unheard of in English soccer circles), play hard and well, and usually win. Then they invited their opponents to the barn. Their girlfriends served snacks, while the boys sought to offer some food for thought.

By this time Madelain's children's club had overflowed her parents' garage, and so she and a friend asked the school principal if they could meet in a classroom at the school. Amazed at such responsible concern in his teenage students, he surprised himself and us by acquiescing. Madelain then asked Angie to start some guitar lessons for her leaders so they could provide some music. Angie complied—immediately connecting with all sorts of weird and wonderful would-be musicians, some with extraordinary talent, and others just plain extraordinary. Those who had joined with hopes of fame in the rock world soon dropped out, but others stayed, forming themselves into groups. They composed their own excellent and moving folk songs of Jesus and His love and helped Angie teach beginners. So started another whole string of events that spread the *Connection* to nearby cities and eventually right across the country.

Angie and I got together to brainstorm our strategy, write music, create dramas, and talk over the development of the children's gifts and artistic abilities. Generally it was a case of gossiping happily over all the good news and happy commotion and plotting to keep pace with it all. Fueled by the Eternal's compelling concern for others, we found a maturity of relationship fashioned between us, respect of each other being born as we handled the daily dilemmas. I decided if I was ever in a really tight spot I would like Angie to be around, not just because she was my friend, but because she kept a cool head and exhibited such comforting *coping* abilities that gave me confidence in crisis.

Some of our older boys had contacts in the local penitentiary, and they asked one of the music groups to have a hymn sing with the men. The day came, and the inmates in that high security prison were marched into the recreation room and told to sit down with their arms folded. Such a captive audience made us amateurs at such efforts in prison ministry nervous. Our master of ceremonies tried to lead the men in the singing of a song, but there was a terrible music generation gap and the results were awful. The prison officer ordered the men to sing—or else—and in desperation John, who was trying to do a good job at being MC, wracked his brain for a song everybody might know.

A Negro spiritual Angie had taught him came to his mind. Without thinking, and not being too sure of the words, he announced, "Let's sing together—'All Your Trials Will Soon Be Over!'" Spontaneous applause and the stamping of feet met his most inappropriate suggestion. Actually it turned out to be the best possible gaffe that could have been made, as the men, roaring with laughter, began to join in the spirit of the meeting and shout out favorite hymns. Soon we were sitting there touched beyond measure, as tears rolled down coarse, scarred cheeks and the strains of "What a Friend We Have in Jesus" rent the state prison air. Music, we found, was the key that would open most of the doors closed to every other method of approach.

Churches started inviting us to take services, and the kids who did the preaching knew they would have to shape up and be different if their testimony was to be viable at all. That inner transformation was always the confirmation that it was God's work taking place and not any pressure we had applied. It never ceased to amaze and delight me to watch someone grow strong when he'd been weak, or sweet when he had been sour, or brave when he had been cowardly, or even clean minded when he had been filthy minded before. I saw it happen over and over again.

It was especially convincing when God changed someone I knew very well. I thought about Julie, who had been my closest friend when

I was little—in fact it was she who helped me organize our village play all those years ago. I had always bossed her about unmercifully. Being a sweet, pliable, and extremely loyal friend, she had patiently allowed me to have my own way—until she had visited us at Capernwray and had come to grips with God in her own still point. Suddenly—and it was certainly a shock to both of us—she started to boss me around. How we giggled about that new strength of personality that entailed such an adjustment. I didn't intimidate her anymore, and she even had the sweet courage to tell me so. I never primed or prompted those reactions in Julie, they just *happened* without anyone saying anything. A sweet new self-assurance had been afforded her, adding a dimension to her self-image she had not enjoyed before. It was this same, solid God-given assurance that motivated the young people to share their newly found confidence in God, and all we had to do was make the contacts with the churches for them.

One night as we returned home with one of our music groups after such a Sunday service, we made the next *Connection*. Needing to relax after an invigorating and challenging time, we stopped for a cup of coffee. It was late at night, but the cafeteria that held about eight hundred people was still full.

"Just look at our captive audience," commented the leader of the music group. Before we could reply, she got up and began to do a wandering minstrel stunt, going from table to table with her guitar, serenading the surprised customers. One or two of them offered her coins, which she ignored, and a few more were downright hostile, but most smiled, and many clapped and asked for more. Others from the music group joined her, and Angie and I tried to hide behind our coffee cups, wondering when the strong hand of the law would descend. Suddenly the manager appeared, and we were not a little relieved to see him smile as he told the group they could continue. He even suggested they might like to return some other weekend to sing to the diners. The kids thought that was a great idea, and so we began to send groups to that cafeteria.

After a few months, our musicians began to feel a little uncomfortable singing about God while people were busy stuffing themselves full of fish and chips; somehow that didn't seem quite reverent or right. So off they went to discuss the situation with their friend the manager, and they came from that interview with the promise of the entire premises for a Folk Festival. We could have our concert around the customers and be allowed to sell tickets and advertise the event. The gang had already decided what they wanted to do with any profit: one of their singers was going to Bible school, and now they knew they could help pay her way. So it was, many surprised travelers wending their way up to the English Lake District found themselves refreshed by a rather different form of background music.

Meanwhile back at Capernwray it was long past time to pull down our barns and build greater. Norman and Anette were about to immigrate to New Zealand, and we needed to leave our old club premises anyway. "What we really need," murmured Angie, "is a central place in the town itself." One of the local boys connected us. Somehow he found out that a huge warehouse was up for sale, and he asked if we wanted to check it out. One quick look was enough for me. It was four stories high with a dead cat lying in the corner of its smelly wet basement. The old stock house had been unused for years, but the grain dust still seemed to be suspended in space. It creaked and groaned with aged dirges, and it sported spooky shadows even in the daylight. There was only one redeeming feature as far as I could see—it was built to last forever. The problem was—I wasn't. I had done enough hard work and knew what it would take to fix up this creaky old building.

"It has *marvelous* possibilities," Angie burbled, all enthusiasm as usual. It did, of course. Charming crooked chimneys linked room to room, while knobbed stone walls and stocky split beams gave a rustic touch. Yes, it certainly had bags of character and endless possibilities for consolidating the whole club work under one roof. Even the Major and Stuart looked at it and thought it was ideal. The boy who told us about it urged me to ask God, but that was the last thing I wanted to do, knowing that *Connections* don't just happen between people and people, but also between people and the Law of the Lord. So many times I had been connected to the relevant word in the Word, and I didn't want to ask *that* at *this* point. In other words, I didn't want my mind changed.

Angie was no help at all as she was busy planning and scheming and in her mind had already moved in. So carefully choosing an unfamiliar portion of the Old Testament, the book of Malachi (for surely there could be nothing helpfully relevant there), I began to read. The book was interesting, having to do with a bunch of religious skinflints who had robbed God. I relaxed somewhat, my conscience being clear on that count. Our tithes had been carefully set aside for God's work. I eventually arrived, however, at Malachi chapter 3, verse 10, and suddenly the hair stood straight up on the back of my neck. It said, "Bring ye all the tithes into the *storehouse,* that there may be meat in mine house, and *prove me now herewith,* saith the Lord of hosts, if I will not open you the windows of heaven, and pour you out a blessing, that there shall not be room enough to receive it."

"Oh no," I muttered weakly, reaching for the phone to relay what I had just read to Angie.

"It's the *Connection,*" she said softly. "We are to *prove Him now.*"

"But all our tithes won't buy it," I argued.

"That's not our business," she answered. "We can't bring more than we have, just *all* we have. Let's go, Jill," she ended urgently. To our amazement the rest of the money was donated, and we found we had a warehouse on our hands.

The day we received the keys, the whole gang of us invaded the premises, exploring the nooks and crevices. We climbed the old wooden ladder into the loft to light some candles (we weren't able to afford electricity) and were led by Angie in some lively, triumphant, foot-stomping songs of victory. As I tussled with a group of guys having fire extinguisher fights and yelled at two more hanging like human bats from the exposed rafters, I was filled with a familiar sense of exhilaration, as if we had somehow come home.

Like all homes, however, there was an awful lot of physical work to be done, and we knew our next responsibility was to ask God to give us the gifts and talents to perform all those tasks. We needed toy building blocks for the nursery school we planned to begin, and the

Eternal sent a young man who worked in a lumber yard and could collect, plane, and polish oddly shaped ends of planks that did the job beautifully. We needed to cover the rough floor boards, and the Lord was already making sure the lovely vinyl flooring would be donated the very same week that the German boy whose trade was installing vinyl flooring arrived at Capernwray. We needed coffee cups and saucers, preferably red and white to match the decor. Somehow things coincided with the redecorating of Forton Café, and the manager gave us his lovely red and white cups and saucers. The cute little nursery chairs we would use were already lined up waiting for us in a nearby playground, having been discarded for newer furniture—a playground that just *happened* to back onto an office block where two of our young people had just been hired.

That very first meeting—sitting close together with the kids in the warm candlelight, the Father encouraged us to ask that it might be given us, to seek that we might find, and to knock that doors of opportunity might be opened to us.

What an education it was going to be for all of us to experience the dramatic *Connections* of prayer! We were to be challenged in the days to come by some of our more cynical observers, who would say to us, "We've seen people helped before at community help centers. So why do you Christians have to credit God with all these arrangements? You're bound to get people who want to do something for a good cause; it's just coincidence, that's all." But the details would tell the story. The *Connections* that consistently happened in answer to our specific requests were too complicated to be explained by coincidence. There was too much evidence that Someone out there was listening.

The bookstore was another case in point. The room we had designed for it formed the corner of the warehouse. It was a funny little crooked spot with angles everywhere and hardly a straight piece of wall in sight. Mary had given up a very nice job to come and, for practically no reimbursement, put the shop into operation. She told me there would be no way we could ever buy shelves to fit that room and that we'd have to have them custom-made. "Oh, Mary," I replied, "we can't afford that."

"Let's pray about it then," she responded. And so in that weird room with piles of books waiting in boxes, we read Malachi 3:10 again. "How about popping some light oak wood bookcases through one of those open windows?" Mary prayed. "And I'd like two of them with glass fronts, please," she added. "All right," He replied, although we didn't hear Him say it. We only knew He must have, because the bookcases arrived from London a week or two later. A lady who had a bookstore of her own, who had never heard of the warehouse or of us, had gone out of business and decided to donate all the stock and furniture to a Christian cause. She wondered just who would want five custom-made light oak bookcases (two with glass fronts) that were all different sizes (her store had been the strangest shape). She chose to ask God about it. Her husband, who was in cattle food, was *connected* with a businessman named Edgar in Lancaster—hundreds of miles away. Edgar happened to have a daughter who came to the warehouse and who knew our needs. Two weeks later the bookcases arrived, fitting perfectly—of course.

And so the old and new endeavors were phased into harmony. The children in the nursery school left me with little time to be lonely, and after a day at nursery school, I was content and slept deeply indeed. Once I fell asleep, the babes pursued me yet, chasing me into rest to play happily in the playground of my mind until the dawning of the day. The climbing frame loomed large, silver gray against a deeply purple sky, with metal-like mobiles of childish shapes clambering in and out. They'd hang and spin and turn completely upside down, then twist and swing suspended by one hand—but never fall. Tinkling laughter like that of a fairy made of joy came flitting through the haze. Did children laugh so much because they remembered better than we did how very happy heaven was? Perhaps that was why babies cried at birth.

My dream meandered on along the halls of memories. Rocking horses raced by thudding and whacking into my night, driven by infant faces without bodies intent on running the race. I wondered which race it was they ran. One of the horses told me as he flew by that he supposed it was the race to ancient age, for what child was there in the whole world who didn't want to be a year older than he was? Sticky, mucky dough appeared oozing out of rolling pins. Children punched and prodded grubby fingers into the mixture, making pies for Mummy to take home. I noticed the little hands got cleaner as the lumps of dough got dirtier. Faces, toys, and colors merged together and became strange translucent letters of the alphabet joining hands with numbers on a counting frame. Hoops were dancing with bats and balls, while ropes turned into snakes wriggling to the rhythm of Indian nursery rhymes played by dolls and teddy bears on toy drums.

I woke with the dawn, and warm reality changed distorted images into clarity. It was time to look at solid substances—like the alarm clock, which tinnily informed me it was time to wake and start again. Lying still under the covers, sorting out the fantasies, I asked myself how I could ever have time to be lonely with day *and* night so thoroughly occupied.

Once the evening had come and our own family had been romped, read to, and readied for their journey into deep fantasy, as God's renewal went to work preparing them for their next day, it was time for Angie and me to head out to play with other children. Perhaps it would be a music class or a visit with a parent's parent. Maybe a painting or a cleaning chore would take the evening, till midnight called us home. It could be that a child was into danger, or beyond it into drugs or drink, and that help was badly needed by police or welfare officers.

Sometimes when Stuart had been briefly home, Angie would take him to the airport returning with last-minute instructions scribbled by my husband on napkins from the coffee shop. Leaving her to do her work, I'd set out by myself, and yet strangely *never alone,* for was not Eternal friendship on my side?

It was on one such night, as I was pushing in and out of crowded promenades in "holiday town" looking for needy teens to whom I could minister, that I met Paul. He was dressed in black, even to the long silk gloves and dark opaque glasses. I asked him why he was so somberly attired and he replied ominously, "So I can *merge* into the shadows." We talked. He was pretty evasive, and I didn't feel comfortable with him. When he turned up at the club I noticed at once the other kids didn't feel safe with him either.

Paul proudly presented us with two big speakers to amplify our music. They looked very new and very hot, and when we inquired where he got them he told us not to ask questions. Angie and I decided we needed to get rid of him, as we were concerned about what he might do to the other teens (and to us!), but just how were we going to do that? Two women were no match for Paul. But after finding a disparity in the coffee shop's accounts, we plucked up enough courage to ask him to go.

That evening he began playing games with me. It was night time and I'd locked up the house when he began to knock on one window after another. When I called for help he would hide and the search party would find nothing. In the end I called the police. It was dark and wintry, and the one and only policeman who served our cluster of country villages lived four miles away. I asked him to come and remove the boy as he was frightening all of us. "What's he done?" he asked.

"Nothing yet," I replied, "but I suspect he's just out of jail."

"Well, I can't do anything to him until he's made a move," he answered. I told him I didn't think *I* could make a move to call him back with a knife sticking out of me, but he replied he couldn't come anyway as he only had his bike, lived miles away—and the wind was against him.

So much for the arm of the law, I thought, as I put down the phone. But I'd read about another arm—an Eternal one. Opening the Law of the Lord, I read, "He that keepeth Israel shall neither slumber nor sleep." It seemed to me the Father was reassuringly saying, "Good night, Jill, *there's no point both of us staying awake.*" And so kept—I slept. Leaning heavily on that unseen support I was able to go to bed, hushing my fears asleep, and leave Paul tapping on the windows. Eventually Stuart returned home and summarily ordered Paul out of our lives, for which we were *more* than grateful.

One night many months later as I was sitting by the fire at home, I felt strangely *released.* It was a new sensation, and I cast about in my mind wondering what it was all about. Angie came in, kicking off her shoes and warming her toes by the blaze. For the next hour she told her heavy concerns for some aspects of the work that needed special attention. I listened to myself agreeing with her conclusions and offering to help her. We looked at each other, for something was happening neither of us fully understood. It was as if she was taking the lead, and I was content to follow. She had become burdened for the operation, at the same time I was becoming free, as though my work was done.

Thousands of miles away across the Atlantic Ocean, Stuart got off a plane in Milwaukee, Wisconsin, to be met by the pastor of the church where he was due to have special meetings. The church's name was *Elmbrook,* and little though we knew it—*there was about to be a new Connection for us all.*

To Be a Friend:
Application and Journal

. . . .

1. Do you have a best friend? (Contrary to popular belief, most women don't.) How important is it to you that you have such a friend? What do you consider valuable traits for a best friend?

2. Which of the following terms do you think your friends would use to describe you?

forgiving	trustworthy	thoughtful	loyal	honest
supportive	good listener	faithful	creative	fun
trusting	affectionate	jealous	insecure	angry
gossip	manipulative	humorless	inflexible	

How would you rate yourself as a friend?

3. What friendships of yours have failed or withered in the past ten years? Why? Do you have a pattern of vulnerability to a particular kind of harmful friendship (controlling, abusive, possessive, or one-sided)?

4. What do your successful friendships have in common? If you have not had many, consider the relationship that has given you the most satisfaction. (It may have been a childhood friendship or one with a relative.) What worked? How can you build on that success in future relationships—without smothering them or holding inflexible expectations?

....

For Action:
If you have not had many close friendships, seek out an older woman, perhaps in your church, who has been successful in friendship and ask her to "mentor" you in friendship. Tell her you want her to be honest when she sees you doing self-defeating things. If you do have several close friends, analyze your relationships. Is there someone on the "outside" who seems to want your friendship?

....

Chapter Nine

....

Mary

....

I'm resigning to join the Capernwray staff," said the minister of Elmbrook Church, as he and my husband traveled out on the freeway toward Brookfield.

"Have you told your people yet?" asked Stuart.

"No," was the reply.

"Then I suggest you wait until after my week's meetings are through, or else no one will listen to a thing I say."

Pastor Hobson agreed to do just that. The meetings went well; the congregation was eager to learn and receptive to this Englishman's style of teaching. At the end of the week, the resignation was announced. Before Stuart boarded a plane for his next assignment, he was approached by a deacon and asked if he would be interested in taking the pastorate. "I'm convinced you are the man for us," he said earnestly, "and we will be praying about it." It was to be the *Connection*.

It was time for a change, that was for sure. I had ceased to be both the mother and father the children needed. It wasn't that I wasn't willing. The plain fact was that I wasn't *able* anymore, and our little ones were showing definite signs of the strain of living without their daddy. Judy sleepwalked, beginning the night after Stuart left for a trip and stopping the night he got back. David failed an important exam at school—making his "I need Father" statements in silent, stubborn behavior patterns that totally changed as soon as his father was around again.

I began to struggle anew with the months of separation that seemed to have no foreseeable end. This time it was not a battle in my spirit, but trauma in my relationships with the children that took me down into depression. David and I were having a war every day, or so it seemed. The battle would begin over nothing and rage on until he retreated to a defensive silence, while I would continue to rant and rave at him for a full five minutes, achieving absolutely nothing except a sick feeling in the pit of my stomach and a spoiled day. Things deteriorated until I found myself walking around the house shutting all the windows "before" the yelling began, as I didn't want the Bible school students to hear me.

It was obvious that something, although I had no idea what, *had* to be done. Although unaware of it at the time, I had not been able to relax or play with Dave for months. I was totally absorbed with the tussle of the moment and the anticipation of the daily parry and thrust of will and words. One morning sitting in the kitchen, totally sick at heart, a horrible thought pushed itself into my mind. Popping its head around the corner of my thinking, it sniped, "You really *dislike* your own child, you know." As I tried to slam the door of denial on it, it insisted, "Yes, you do—you do—*you do!*"

"But I *love* David," I screamed at the slimy, suggestive thing. "I love him, I do—I do—I *do!*" Forced to face reality, however, I had to admit the accusation was at least partially right. Amid a flood of guilty, desperate tears, I wondered miserably if my son was aware of my feelings. I didn't know it was possible to *love* someone but sometimes not to like him very much. The things I disliked about Dave at that particular stage were the very things he didn't like about me.

No one had explained that most parents have some such personality conflict with one child or another, and that usually the clashes occur with the individual most like themselves. And so not having learned that elementary piece of psychology, I beat and lectured myself, mourning the bitterness between us and worrying that the hostilities would never cease. The inevitable result was a bleeding ulcer that wreaked internal havoc as I tried to forget my troubles by taking on an increased workload.

It was at this point that Stuart wrote the letter telling me that Elmbrook Church had invited him to be their pastor. He wanted me to pray about it. *How was I expected to do that?* I thought somewhat desperately. Someone was offering us the chance to spend time together as a *real* family during our children's teenage years, and he was asking me to *pray* about it? I could hardly believe such a marvelous opportunity had come our way. My husband would be able to take over the discipline of our son, and I would be able to rebuild that broken bridge of friendship and understanding between us. Knowing it was not possible to be objective, I requested the Eternal find someone less biased to do the praying for me, wondering meanwhile how I would stay willing for either alternative—America or England.

A few weeks later it became apparent that the move to the United States was indeed the right thing to do—"For Stuart and the children, you mean," I snapped at God. I had become so ill I couldn't hide it any longer. Angie took it into her own hands to call the doctor, who had me in the hospital within hours. They began testing everything in and out of sight. Not knowing yet about the ulcer, I was convinced God had brought me there to stop me from being a hindrance to my husband and a thorn in the side of my son. I had come to the morbid conclusion that I was going to die. This way, I reasoned, Stuart could be given an American wife to match his job, and my son would have a mother who could relate to him.

I had forgotten that the devil is not a gentleman and that he had kicked me before when I was down and alone. I was also too exhausted to remember that Satan is the accuser of the brethren—in this case the "sisteren"—and when he can't get others to do his work for him, he will encourage us to accuse ourselves. How very miserable and how very sure I was that I would never make it across the sea to America.

Turning to the Eternal's Law without really expecting help, I stumbled across the story of Elijah. His energies spent and psychologically and spiritually beaten, he ran away from his responsibilities and requested that he might die. Even Elijah, the great and mighty prophet, felt like I did. I was sure he would be in for a good "it's time to straighten up, man" talk from Jehovah. But no. Reading on, I saw that he received only the tenderest *touch* and the kindest of words: "Arise and eat; because the journey is too great for thee" (1 Kings 19:7). The application was almost too obvious. I knew He saw me, in that hospital, beaten, defeated, and totally spent. He had sent His words to touch me even as He touched Elijah, and He told me in love: "The journey is too great for thee"; sleep, eat, and get well again—and then we'll see about the United States.

I slept deeply for the first time in weeks, having been delivered from the "My husband would be better off without me" syndrome and encouraged to be ready to believe again that I was the right wife for Stuart and the only mother David wanted. The ulcer found, and medication given, the move was planned and I set about packing.

One of the hardest things for me to do was to say good-bye to my mother. "How do I do that, Lord, just as she's getting on in years and needs me around?" I asked with an aching heart. "And how about the fact that she won't have the joy of watching her grandchildren grow up, and what happens when she's sick and old and I'm thousands of miles away?" Yes, it was going to be terribly hard to look Peggy in the eyes and tell her I was going to live such a long distance from her— probably for the rest of her life. I was being torn in pieces—for my family was scattered all over the place and I couldn't go or stay without the sharp knife of distance severing part of me.

Suddenly the most ordinary things became almost sacred in their importance, appearing desperately dear and even charming in their function. For example, the red buses roaring up and down the town seemed to be saying cheekily, "Ride us, Jill, you'll not find us over there in the good old United States." How was it I had never noticed before how the neat hedges properly confined the woolly lambs and lazy black-and-white checkered cows? The demure, hand-fashioned gray slate walls suddenly told me to etch their shapes into my memory bank, as if they knew there would be no boundaries privatizing our property or our lives in Brookfield, Wisconsin.

The brass letter box that daily opened its friendly mouth to gulp our letters down became another of the ridiculous and dear parts of English paraphernalia I would find myself missing as I journeyed across my "yard" instead of "garden" to collect the "mail," rather than the "post" from those crude tin cylinders stuck on raw, wood sticks. These and so many more familiar, funny things triggered that strange, unexplainable homesickness way beyond the "allowable" adjustment period. Writing them all deeply into my heart, I took my final walks and those long, last looks around my country—my England.

The good-byes were spluttered out, the hot tears spilled, the sweet mother kisses given, and that willing, gentle, giving spirit manifested as Peggy sent me on my way to be part of the life of the man I loved and had lived apart from for so very, very long. "Your place is at his side," she said quietly and determinedly, and added wistfully, "Come back and see us whenever you can."

And so that was how in the month of November, nineteen hundred and seventy, we found ourselves coming "home" to Brookfield, Wisconsin—for "home is the will of God," you know.

At first it was all like a happy, happy dream, and I kept thinking I would wake and find it all a fantasy. I couldn't get used to the idea that I wasn't on vacation and it would not soon be time to return to the familiar situation and the faces that had been part of our lives for so long. I had never heard of culture shock and so had no way of knowing that's what we were all suffering from, in one form or another, but it was quite a pleasant malady and didn't upset us too much as the days went by.

I was far too shy to ask all the questions I wanted to ask, but the strange phenomena needed to be interpreted. The children had no such qualms, so I would tell them to ask my questions at school and get all my queries answered there. "Why do so many people want to sell their garages?" I puzzled, passing yet another "garage sale" notice. "And why do people keep inviting me to a 'shower' when we have three bathrooms in our own house?"

The recipes I tried to make came out all wrong as the scales I had been used to were replaced with measuring cups. I discovered the butter was too salty, the sugar too fine, and the flour quite strange indeed. But English "puddings" had to make way for American pies, and we needed to adjust to eating raw vegetables as well as cooked ones. David balked at mixing sweet and savory foods together all on one plate. McDonald's took over from the fish-and-chip shops, and I soon got used to calling biscuits cookies; chips, french fries; crisps, potato chips. We learned that English muffins (though I had never seen them in England) were good for breakfast. I was told the bonnet and boot of my car were really the hood and the trunk, and I needed to go on the highway not the freeway—and if we were walking the dog we should stay on the sidewalk not the pavement. Soon our new vocabulary was almost complete.

Meanwhile, Prince, our beautiful golden retriever, was undergoing his own form of culture shock, being somewhat bewildered as he found he needed to be confined to a chain and the sheep and cows he had chased at will had mysteriously disappeared. We did let him out late at night. Having been tied up all day and being a retriever, he would run furiously around the neighborhood, collect all the door-mats he could find, and pile them neatly outside our back door. I would have to wait till midnight and then set off to return them all, trying to match up the size and shape to the steps or patio.

Shortly after immigrating and before we had been able to register him, Prince went AWOL. We had arrived in winter, just in time for the first snowfall, and the children were terribly upset thinking their dog's feet would freeze and they would never see him again. That night they asked God to keep him safe and bring him back to us. I was not so hopeful after two whole days had passed and there had been no signs of the animal, when suddenly a man appeared at the door with Prince. He told us the police had picked him up and taken him to the pound (not English money, I learned, but the dog home). Since he still had his English identification tag, they had tried to contact the name on it, which simply said, "WRAY HALL"—the "Capern" part of the first word having worn off. Mr. Wray Hall was duly found in the phone book and discovered to be our next-door neighbor, who knew we had lost our dog. How's that for a *Connection* in a city of a million people! I'm sure the Eternal knew how important that animal was to three newly adjusting English kids and saw to it their prayer was answered.

One morning a kind new friend invited me to go to "My Fair Lady" with her. She was an actress, and I was quite excited to see an American rendering of the play. It did strike me as slightly strange that I was to be picked up at 9 A.M., and I was not a little puzzled when she told me she went twice a week. *Was the American theater's repertoire really so limited?* I wondered. When she arrived, I was even more amazed to see that American ladies wore black leotards for the occasion. I must admit I felt somewhat overdressed, having spent careful time preparing for a theater visit. Being sweetly polite, my friend said nothing about my smart attire, but wended her way to the exercise parlor bearing the name "My Fair Lady" over the entrance.

As the settling-in continued, we began to send reports home to our families and friends concerning all the marvelous things we were experiencing, and it wasn't long before I was hoping some of them could come and visit us. Week after week I dutifully wrote to my mother-in-law. Every now and then my husband dropped her a line as well. One day I said to Stuart, "Darling, why don't you write your mother a long letter this week? She'd much rather hear from you once than ten times from me." And so he sat down and corresponded with Mary, and I had a week off.

After a few days the reply came, and since Stuart was out of town I opened it. It started, "Darling Stuart, how *wonderful* to get such a lovely long newsy letter from you and yes, I would *love to come and stay for three months.*" As I absorbed that electric piece of information, I made up my mind not ever to let Stuart write to his mother again.

Three months! Now I would have to get around to putting a few things together. Sitting there with the letter in my hand, I thought about Mary. Stuart had wanted me to meet his parents almost as soon as we met, and I knew it meant a lot to him that we liked each other. I remembered walking toward his parents' home, a smart black-and-white gabled house perched coyly among impeccably kept rose beds and trim English lawns, in the town of Kendal in the English Lake District. I couldn't help noticing the windows. They shone, brilliantly reflecting the late afternoon sun, and looked as though someone had just finished washing and polishing them that very minute. Stuart and his brother, Bernard, teased Mary that she spent her time standing in the middle of a room with the dustpan in her hand waiting to catch the dust before it ever dared settle on her furniture.

Polish! That was my first impression. Highly polished mahogany wood, highly polished beautiful brassware, a highly polished kitchen, and I swear even the pebbles on the walkway outside looked highly polished too. Mary's house reflected her grim determination to wage war with dirt and dullness and make it all shine.

The letter fluttered in my hand as I glanced guiltily around my kitchen. Why hadn't I ever noticed those finger marks all over my freezer? But I really knew why I hadn't been conscious of them until now—Mary was coming. I thought about her tall, stately figure, sitting in the lovely Queen Anne chair, with her spine as stiff as a ramrod and her ankles neatly crossed (because her mother had always told "the girls" to put their backs right into the base of the chair and sit up "properly"). Stretching my back from its slouchy posture, I began to practice—for Mary was coming. I remembered visiting her for afternoon tea one day and asking where some obscure item we needed was kept, and she sent me directly to it. As I brought it forth Mary smiled with satisfaction, saying, "My mother always taught me the secret of good housekeeping is that *everything* has a place." *Well,* I thought somewhat defensively, *everything in our house has a place as well—it's just that they aren't kept there most of the time.*

"Grandma"—Mary's mother—was a character in her own right, and I loved her the moment I met her. Maybe that was because I had never known a grandmother of my own, but she loved me too and even decided to come and stay with us for a little vacation. We had a problem with the heating while she was there, but she was determined not to go home until her allotted time was up, even though we were all convinced she'd get her death of cold.

The visit took place just after Stuart's father had died, and "Gran" had come to stay with us to be near while Mary put her papers in order after the funeral. While she was with us, a really funny incident occurred. Stuart's mum had never learned to drive, but now at retirement age, she decided if she was ever going to be able to live by herself she had better pass her test. "Quite right, Mary," Gran encouraged her—"get our Bernard to teach you." "Our Bernard" was happy enough to teach his mother, although the two being very much alike they were a little like flint and steel if ever they spent too much time in close proximity.

Mary had a lodger, a German boy who had been renting a room in her house. He had been a tremendous comfort and help to her since Pop had died, and we were all glad he was there. As long as they kept off the subject of German–British relations they got on just famously. The day of Mary's first driving lesson started off, however, with a TV special of the European soccer final, which featured Germany playing England. The German's pride rose to the occasion, and he was crowing with glee over a goal when Mary cut him down to size by snapping at him, "Well, now Abehart, just remember we've beaten you twice at your favorite national sport."

Looking rather surprised, Abehart asked, "Which sport is that?"

"War!" said Mary. So saying she put on her hat and swept outside into the car with the young man following her, understandably not a little put out. Having impeccable Aryan manners, however, and as Mary needed a qualified driver sitting beside her to get to Bernard's house, he did not allow his personal feelings to stop him from keeping his promise to go with her.

It was pouring when they arrived. Bernard wasn't at all sure this was the best of days to start to teach his mother to drive. It was also Sunday and traffic was heavy. "I can't wait," Mary said impatiently as he began to reason with her. "Get in, Bernard, and we'll drive to Jill's so I can see my mother."

Off they set with Bernard greeting Abehart, who had moved somewhat nervously into the backseat. "I like your suit," Bernard told him.

"It's new," replied Abehart, glad of the distraction as he had been trying not to look at the distorted shapes flying by the windows at a rather alarming rate. Mary literally charged along the narrow country lanes.

Bernard tried to give her some advice, which she appeared to ignore. He then began to tell her what to do in an authoritarian voice. In the end, when she either didn't do it or didn't know what he meant her to do, she said, "Bernard, stop talking to me like that or get out!"

"I'll get out then, thank you," said he. It was absolutely deluging down and they were at least two miles away, but true to his word Bernard got out of the vehicle, shut the door, and began to walk toward our house. Mary was mad.

Sitting in the back seat, Abehart was aghast. He decided he had better get out of the car and move into the front. Mary misunderstood his intention and said to herself, *I never thought Abehart would leave me alone!* Recovering quickly, she decided, *Well, now that's all right— they can BOTH walk, if that's what they want,* and off she went roaring down that English country road as if her life depended on it, leaving poor Abehart standing in the storm in his brand-new Sunday suit.

We were all pretty surprised to see Mary arrive alone, but she swept in and related the whole story to Gran and me. About half an hour later the two drowned rats appeared. Abehart's face was an absolute picture, and I had a good idea what he was about to say, but before he could get a word out, Gran rose to her feet, grabbed a cushion, and boxed him over the ears with it saying, with grandmotherly indignation, "Fancy leaving our Mary all on her own like that—you ought to be ashamed of yourself!"

With fantastic and commendable self-control, Abehart silently turned on his heel and disappeared to change into one of Stuart's suits, the body language of his disappearing back saying it all.

All those charged personalities, and all that gritty character wrapped up in just one family, I thought, laughing in the midst of my memories. Gran was such a character it was no wonder Mary had inherited many of her great strengths. And now she was coming to stay—for *three* months!

Well, it shouldn't be too hard, I thought. She had lived with us before, after she had had her first heart attack. In fact, I had prided my-self on being the member of the family who got on best with her—simply because I had decided to keep my distance, let her have her way, and adopt an "anything for peace" attitude. Mary was very con-servative, that was all, and if one could respect her point of view and agree to disagree, then one could live with it—even for three months. Besides, I loved her, and I didn't just love her because she gave me Stu-art. I loved her because she gave me Mary too, and Mary was so many gifts wrapped into one great package. For one thing, she was the gift of brave example, for she had shown me how to suffer. Unknown to me at that point, she would also show me how to die.

It would be a great joy to introduce her to all our wonderful friends, I concluded, knowing from my own happy experience how phenomenally good and generous the church would be to her and how thrilled she would be to see the way God was blessing her son's ministry. I knew there would be no problem at all with the three chil-dren; they would love showing off all their new American things to their grandma. I just didn't know about us. About Mary and me. Up to now we had loved at a distance and privately, but now we were to love up close—and in public—and for that I needed some time in the still point.

The Law of the Eternal was ready with a good example for me. Turning to the portion of Scripture that showed a mother-in-law/daughter-in-law relationship, I read the book of Ruth, perusing the story of Naomi. She had left Bethlehem with her husband and boys and ended up in a foreign land with her two daughters-in-law. Her menfolk had died, leaving her lonely and bitter. When she an-nounced her plans to return home, Orpah and Ruth impulsively de-cided to go along.

It was not hard for me to get the message. Naomi represented Mary, who had been left alone by her menfolk. Mary had not been without her bitter moments—even as Naomi—but it had not stopped me from loving her or her from loving me. It was just that up to now I had been content to be an Orpah. She was the girl who went "so far" and no further with their relationship. When the crunch came she turned back to go her own way. Naomi didn't try to stop her; in fact she encouraged her to go, fondly kissing her good-bye. She laid no obligation on Orpah, as Mary had laid no obligation on me. There was a good enough relationship between us; for Mary had never demanded anything more than I had given.

But was "a good enough relationship" good enough? I knew the answer to that question before I ever asked it, for I knew I was being instructed and commanded by the example given by Ruth. "Intreat me not to leave thee, or to return from following after thee," she had said, "for whither thou goest, I will go; and where thou lodgest, I will lodge: thy people shall be my people, and thy God my God: Where thou diest, will I die, and there will I be buried: the Lord do so to me, and more also, if ought but death part thee and me" (Ruth 1:16–17). I was terribly convicted by Ruth's determination to identify, for the Bible said, "When she [Naomi] saw that she [Ruth] was *stedfastly minded* to go with her," the arguments ceased. "So they two went . . ." (vv. 18–19, italics added).

It all seemed so dramatically relevant, as it was obvious that Ruth's choice was the identification the Eternal was asking of me. My house, Mary's house; Mary's people, my people. I was to respect and accept her conservative cultural background, which was foreign to me, and I was to serve her in submissive love, for her God was my God. He would make the difference. It wasn't a case of a class or church barrier this time; it was bigger than all of that—this was certainly one of the biggest barriers of all—the mother-in-law barrier. My part was surely going to need determination that would not be a matter of the emotions—but a matter of the will. "I *will* go," said Ruth. "I *will* lodge . . . I *will* die and there *will* I *be buried!*" "I" was surely going to have to be buried for it to all work out.

When I told my church friends that Mary was coming, they were most interested—too interested. I found myself wanting to march around the house, not to shut the windows this time, but to draw the drapes and say, "Leave me to struggle this one through alone." But again He stopped me short. "When Naomi and Ruth came home to

Bethlehem, it wasn't private," God reminded me. "In fact, My Word says, when they came home together the whole city was moved."

Well now, that's a switch, I thought. We don't need Billy Graham to move a city—just some mothers-in-law loving their daughters-in-law and vice versa—that'll do it. I thought of all the awful mother-in-law jokes I had heard down the years—why, only that week, a friend had told me his mother-in-law had come to visit but she was leaving on the four o'clock broom. I wanted an altogether new and kinder attitude.

The visit started off marvelously well. The children couldn't wait to take Grandma to a different eating place each day. In England we hardly ever went out to eat because there were few fast-food restaurants and it was too expensive. How Mary loved this special American treat! Taco Bell, Pancake House, Arby's, and, of course, McDonald's were all sampled. Mary, like a child let out of school, reveled in each new sight, sound, taste, and smell. Every night after dinner, the ice cream parlor was a "must." We planned thirty-two visits to make sure we would get to sample *all* the flavors. She had her photo taken holding a beautiful pumpkin, and she collected the gorgeous autumn maple leaves to press in her vacation diary. We were having a ball!

And then it happened. A suspicious, frightening lump was discovered! Twenty-two years previously the first lump had been removed. Cancer had been faced, fought, and prayed into submission. Now it was back. I ran to my room, opened the book of Ruth, and read those verses over again with a new awareness. God had been preparing me— "Where thou diest I will die and there will I be buried."

Sitting in that downtown hospital listening to our doctors telling us as gently as they knew how that "this was it," I found myself refusing to accept the information they were giving me. "Mary must stay in your home," they were saying, "and we'll take care of her together."

"No!" I shouted inside. "What about our children—I don't want them to see death that close up—not yet." My mother had always sought to shield me from the trauma of death, and I wanted to do the same for them.

"It will be a good experience for the children," our doctor was assuring us, as if he had read my unspoken objections. "Mary needs the family now."

"No," I screamed again internally. "I can't do it. I can't be the Florence Nightingale people will expect me to be." I was scared of the decay and the mess and the nursing, and my mind scurried away to the terrible details of my father's deathly disintegration.

As I looked around at the group with a growing horror of anticipation, I felt trapped. How could I possibly tell Stuart how I was feeling? Surely he would be terribly hurt. I knew the thing that was expected of me was something only I could do for Mary—and for my husband—and yet here I was wrestling with such selfish and childish reactions.

Later I talked it over with my doctor. "You're the only one who knows how I feel," I told him—and then I whispered, "I don't want her to die here."

"Well," he replied quite calmly, "you're doing fine, for you've been able to admit it. You are passing through the perfectly normal phase of rejection, and I believe you'll soon climb right through to acceptance."

But I didn't feel the rejection of my responsibilities was normal. Where were the marvelous Christian attitudes I had dreamed about in the past as I had pictured such a situation arising? What about all those great sermons concerning love and sacrifice I had been giving? And how was I going to hide my struggle from Mary, for hide it I knew I must? "God help her never to know I ever harbored such thoughts," I prayed, "and change me." Words that Major Thomas had preached years ago at Capernwray came to mind. He had been speaking about God's sufficiency in the face of our inadequacy, and he told us the Lord was never surprised or panicked by our natural reactions. He used a little couplet concerning the Eternal's expectations that had remained with me . . .

You can't—I never said you could
I will—I always said I would!

And there it was. Just what I needed when I needed it.

God expected nothing from me but failure. His power would transform my attitudes and make me "un-me"-like all over again.

The next day I sat down with Mary, took her hand in mine, looked into her eyes, and in obedience to God said, "Mary, I want you to stay with us to the end." She didn't see my heart, she only heard the words, and she never knew that the victory was only half won. The words were said, and the emotions caught up with them in a few weeks, for that is how the love life of God works. If you do the works of love before the emotions match up, the feelings of love will eventually follow along.

The daily cobalt was administered for a whole three months; the sickness and pain followed; but oh, in the midst of it, there was blessing to us all. Did we ever see such courage! The day came when the treatments were finished. "Mrs. Briscoe," said the nurse to Mary, "very few people live to see the end of these treatments, and certainly not without tears. You did both!"

"What's the use of crying?" responded Mary spiritedly. "Tears don't help." The nurse looked at me, awed into wondering silence.

"Women are made to suffer," Mary said cheerfully, settling back in the car. Now it was to get harder—as the cat-and-mouse waiting began. Where would the dread thing appear next, and what would have to be taken out, cut off, or burned into oblivion the next time? All we could do was to be patient and appreciate the good days.

There were duties I had to see to and meetings I needed to take that necessitated my being out of the house for long periods. Sometimes I would come back and hear the creaking of the rocking chair and know that certain sound was telling me I would be living with disapproval for a while. It must have been terribly difficult for Mary, used to an impeccable house, to watch me leaving things I decided were "less important" than the "most important" things in my schedule. She never verbalized her frustrations to me, and I was so thankful she apparently forgave me all of it as we worked at accepting each other as we were.

Eighteen months and two operations later, Mary was spent. It was going to get very rough from now on. I remember taking my Bible into the still point to get a little light on some big decisions. There were engagements ahead that needed to be canceled, and I needed to face the end with Mary.

I went back to the book of Ruth, beginning to read the story where I had left off months before. I couldn't believe my eyes. "I went out full," said Naomi, *"and the Lord hath brought me home again empty. . . ."* So Naomi returned with Ruth, "and they came to Bethlehem in the beginning of barley harvest" (Ruth 1:21–22, italics added). *She's going home to England,* the Eternal was telling me. *She will die there in her own home, in her own bed, with her own son nursing her into My arms.* And so it was. Just a few days after I had read those very words, Mary told us she wanted to go home to England. And it was the beginning of barley harvest!

Not a week has gone by since she died that we have not remembered or quoted her—smiled or nodded our heads in deep appreciation of the impact she made on all of our lives. Almost daily her name has been on our lips, and her presence lingers in our behavior patterns as I catch myself sitting straight up in my seat, or when I am reminded that every item should have "a place." When my dryer continually eats up one sock of a pair, I think guiltily about the way Stuart or Bernard always had a pair to put on. At family reunions there always comes a point in a friendly argument when one of us will say in "Mary's" voice, "Isn't it nice that we can all be together." Everyone stops quibbling and laughs warmly, knowing she would laugh at herself if she were still among us.

When Pete brings a report card "like his dad's" from school, the time for "Mary" stories begins. Stuart will tell of the time he brought home his straight-A card and all he got from Mother was the comment, "Just see what you could have done if you'd tried." She was right, of course, and that man of mine acknowledges his mother's educational disciplines in his life. He credits her for her part in his achievements, thankful most of all for leading him while still a child to the Christ she loved and served.

Yes, Mary was strong; Mary was powerfully straight and true and above all brave right to the end. The doctors couldn't believe how she lingered on, having cancer for twenty-two years, enduring three heart attacks and radical surgery. Bernard told us after it was all over, "It was just as if that old angel of death was sitting in the corner of her bedroom for a long time, and she fixed him with a gimlet eye and said, 'You can wait till *I'm* ready!'" We laughed, for that was Mary. It wasn't that she wasn't ready to go—she was, for she dearly loved the Lord. In fact, when Stuart had told his plans and preparations for his visit to the Holy Land, she had smiled indulgently and said, "Well, enjoy yourself. I'm going to the New Jerusalem." In the words of Paul, her life had been lived that she might know Him, *the power of His resurrection, and the fellowship of His sufferings.* How grateful to God I was for the privilege of watching it all close up.

It was time now to turn my attention to being a pastor's wife. I thought back to my initial adjustment period a couple of years before when I arrived in the States and some of the lessons I had learned. Looking around the huge congregation we had come to serve, I had wondered how I could possibly relate.

The only thing I had had to compare the church to were parishes back in England that were so different they may as well have been on Mars. To begin with, the size of the fellowship had been overpowering, especially when I compared it with Stuart's church heritage, and I remembered the first time I had gone along with him to the little meeting hall where the faithful gathered Lord's Day by Lord's Day. There were no ministers; the elders led the worship. Women kept quiet, wore hats, and never wore pants. It was all pretty solemn.

Sitting between Bernard and Stuart on my first visit with my eyes as big as saucers, I had wondered if anybody ever smiled and how on earth I would fit into a place like this. The leader of the meeting had risen to his feet to give the notices and announced that there would be a visiting speaker from another town on the weekend and there would be refreshments served afterward. Pausing, he had looked around and then announced solemnly, "So would the sisters please assemble for cutting up for sandwiches." Both Bernard and Stuart had kept their faces perfectly straight, but managed to dig me in the ribs to make sure I'd got the joke.

Bursting out laughing all on my own, I had to turn it into a cough hastily, glaring at the guys meanwhile for putting me on the spot like that. No, there wasn't a pastor's wife in that group to model myself by, that was for sure. To begin with there wasn't even a pastor.

I had thought next about the pastor's wife from the church we had been married in. Try as I would, I couldn't even remember what she looked like. Someone had told me she believed being a pastor's wife meant she could legitimately opt out of all church responsibilities because she had her vocation cut out for her looking after the pastor. What was I to do and where was I to look for this personage living in the parsonage? Seeing my confusion, would the congregation try a takeover, makeover, rake-over bid, I wondered?

I had to find out first what their expectations were going to be. Beginning to ask around, I encouraged the ladies to tell me what they hoped I would do for them. Returning home with the heavy information, I had made an English cup of tea (which is what one does in times of crisis) and began to think of packing to go back to England. "Jill," Stuart said sharply as I poured out my worried complaints, "if a job's worth doing, it's worth doing badly!"

I had shaken my head frantically. He had it all wrong. "If a job's worth doing, it's worth doing well," I corrected him, and then continued miserably, "and that's the problem. I don't have the gifts to do it well, and I can't come up to people's expectations."

"If a job's worth doing, it's worth doing badly rather than not doing it at all," he repeated patiently, and off he had gone whistling to do his job "well," I was sure.

It's all right for him, I had said grimly to no one in particular. *He's always so relaxed, calm, and capable.* The Eternal's Law lay on the table, and I had opened it in a challenging sort of way as if to say, "Go on, and show me something that says if a job's worth doing, it's worth doing badly." I knew it couldn't possibly have anything like *that* in there. Beginning to read my way through the epistles, seeking some principles or promise that might encourage me, I found some help: "Whatsoever ye do, do it *heartily,* as to the Lord" (Colossians 3:23). Well, at least I could do that, I had decided. And so two years previously I had started to do it heartily and badly.

In the following days, two things began to happen. First, some jobs I had started out by doing badly, I began to do *goodly*. In other words, as I jumped in and tried, I discovered gifts I didn't know I had. The other lesson learned had to do with the duties and responsibilities that I hadn't discovered a gift for. The best I could do with those things was to do them as heartily as I could and as badly as I did. This engendered a most interesting reaction. Some women who had been sitting vegetating in a pew, and who possessed those very abilities that I didn't, would watch my sad efforts, and come to me most sympathetically saying, "Oh, Jill, I think you'd better let us help"—and that was the way I began to get some of the jobs done that needed doing around the place. It had been lots of fun. So I never did have a model of a pastor's wife to copy and it was probably just as well, for I had had to learn to please the Lord—not the ladies—and that had been a huge and necessary stepping-stone to a self-assurance I needed to experience.

The church had grown very quickly. Soon we hired a theater and had a second service there. It was a little unorthodox, but there were many who felt they could put up with the sticky seats, dim lights, and the popcorn on the floor if it meant they could slip in unobserved. People were checking the new English preacher out. They apparently liked what they saw—or rather heard, for as I have already said, the lights were a bit dim.

Four years later a new church building was dedicated, and everyone crowded in to admire the beautiful structure and enjoy the luxury of finding somewhere to park for a change. God was moving in our midst and we rejoiced. As we sped home that night, the radio was playing a typical commercial, "When I hear Milwaukee, I think of beer!" Stuart and I looked at each other. One day when the radio was turned on and people thought of Milwaukee—perhaps the song would end another way.

1. How would you describe your relationship with your mother-in-law? (If you do not have a mother-in-law, think about an aunt, a grandmother, or another relative.)

2. Are you satisfied with a "good enough" relationship? In what areas do you need to work at a deeper level of friendship?

3. In what areas do you find it hard to identify with your mother-in-law? What adjustments have you been reluctant to make? On the other hand, what adjustments have one or both of you made well?

4. What are some everyday traits of your mother-in-law that you have taken for granted, but which make your life easier, more pleasant, or more fun? What less positive traits have encouraged your emotional or spiritual growth (such as patience, forgiveness)?

. . . .

For Action:
Write your mother-in-law (or other relative) a friendly note,
and add "P.S. I don't know if I've ever told you, but I really like
[a trait or consistent action of hers]." Be sure it is not worded
to look like you are asking for something from her.

. . . .

Chapter Ten

The Ultra-Suede Ladies

I had tea with the queen," the beautiful lady informed me. "Queen who?" I wanted to ask facetiously. But I knew "who"—Queen Elizabeth, of course—my queen. This beautiful, polished American lady was to share the platform with me at a women's retreat. After describing her tea party with the Queen of England in detail, she added another story of yet one more "queenly" interview in another European capital, where she had been able actually to talk to "Her Majesty" about the Lord.

Settling back in the big black limousine that was speeding us toward the retreat center, I dreamed my dreams that had been fanned by my companion's stories. I had never even seen *"my"* queen in the flesh, never mind had tea with her. How absolutely marvelous! I envisioned myself in Buckingham Palace, standing in a huge room under a gigantic chandelier, holding a white Bible in my hand. I would wear a seraphic smile as I talked about the still point. I would know *just* the "right" thing to say to the royal relatives and be in complete charge of myself—and the situation.

Carried away with such fantasies, I could see the words "Reach a Royal for Christ" written across the sunset. Then the connections would be bound to begin, I thought. The Royal Guards would soon

bow their black fuzzy hats in prayer as they stood in their compact little boxes outside the palace gates. I was brought back to earth (or even
lower) by the beautiful lady asking, "And just where have *you* been
speaking lately?"

I gazed at her, completely lost for words. I wanted to say casually,
"Oh, Washington, D.C., a little Bible study meeting with the con-
gressmen's wives, and then on to the Florida Hilton, before dropping
in for a quick meeting at the governor's mansion." I wanted to say it
because all of those invitations had been given to me, but I couldn't,
because not all those opportunities had been taken. Looking at my
beautiful ultra-suede companion, I felt the old familiar struggle all
over again. *I wanted to be like her.*

Ultra-suede ladies frightened me out of my mind. I don't mean
just the ultra-suede ladies, but the *ultra, ultra* ones! They threatened
me, and I had already decided there was absolutely no way that God
could use me to reach "the up and outers." I mean, "just look at me," I
mumbled miserably as I slumped against the upholstery in a self-conscious heap.

Here I was in my forties, suffering the teenage bad self-image syndrome. I wanted to shout at my Maker, "Why don't you recall all
those 1935 models with defects and make us right? For a start, you
could give me new hair." It had never grown up and "become adult."
It was the fine baby type that convinced me I faced premature bald-
ness. To look nice when I was traveling and "on show" all the time and
at all hours (with no time to curl and primp my lank locks) meant I
had to sit bolt upright in an airplane seat for hours on end. If I leaned
back, my hair flattened into a pancake. After all, I had to look pre-
sentable for the reception committee waiting at the airport. It was
tempting to stand in line and get on the plane with a plastic bag over
my head so the wind wouldn't mess up the "image."

It was years before I could travel comfortably in some suitable apparel and employ the time to rest and relax. It was a long time before I
discovered the advantages of having a bad publicity shot taken (I'm
very unphotogenic—I hope). This way when people meet me at the
airport clutching my photo for identification (and the orchid designed

for disintegration) they are pleasantly surprised when they see me and say with obvious relief, "Oh, you're a *lot* prettier than your picture!" (I have long since discovered it is also a sensible idea to travel in a jean suit. It prevents you from being pinned painfully to your orchid; after all, it doesn't really look right on denim.) But sitting in the speeding limousine, I was nervous about playing the role and trying to look the part of the traveling lady speaker.

Not only would I have liked to have asked the Eternal why He had not given me strong, wavy, stay-in-place hair, to go with the job in hand, but I also mulled over the question of why He hadn't made my metabolism so that I could eat all those sweet, sticky, energy-giving cakes and hot fudge sundaes that I wanted and still stay slim and trim. I found myself starving after each speech, craving an extra shot of energy to meet a demanding traveling schedule. Usually I was far too nervous to eat before I spoke, and after shaking hundreds of hands at the conclusion of the meeting I would turn around just in time to see my dinner being tossed into the garbage pail. Then all that was left for me to do was to wander along to the coffee shop and eat all the wrong things, which would then appear in all the wrong places.

When I stayed in a private home, people were just too kind in their care of me. How do you refuse your hostess's lovingly prepared caloric recipes without offending her? And anyway, who wants to refuse? I certainly didn't, especially down South, where I found myself eating my way through the Chattanooga cookbook. Glancing sideways in the semi-dark cab, I acknowledged the super-trim shape of my companion with something akin to gloom and despair. How would one ever gain the ear of the ultra, ultra-suede ladies unless she looked like a size-eight model?

"And then, Lord, there is the money problem." How could I ever afford to dress ultra-suede to match my audience, or on the other hand how would I cope with the trouble arising if I did? For one thing, the ultra, ultra-suede who seemed to put such store in appearance mightn't listen if I didn't match up dresswise, but then the "sub-suede" in the audience (like me!) might consider an ultra-suede outfit a gross misuse of the Lord's money.

I remembered with a shudder the time I found myself a guest in an incredible villa. We were to change for dinner in a "small" bedroom (about half the size of our entire house). The other ladies were pouring themselves into their exclusive outfits and throwing around the casual remarks about Dior's latest show. It was my turn in the shower, and, grateful for the respite, I spent so long in there my skin began to get quite waterlogged. Miserably reaching for the gorgeous bath towel and wondering momentarily if that wouldn't look better than my dress, I tried tying it around myself "sari" style. It was certainly cute and different, but I knew it wouldn't do, so reluctantly I had to emerge wrapped in the terrific terry cloth toga, with my little bit of starched cotton dress hanging limply from my hand.

I was met by a fabulous-looking creature who remarked kindly, "That looks like a pretty little creation, Jill." She had focused the attention of the entire roomful of women onto my apparel. I didn't need to say it, but I did anyway. "Sears," I whispered, as if I'd just been caught shoplifting. *Why did I do that?* I asked myself furiously. Why couldn't I just smile and say "thank you"? It *was* a pretty dress and quite as lovely as all the rest, just not as expensive. I knew in my heart, of course, that my reaction was a guilty confession to these women that because of the way I looked I felt totally out of place among them.

At that moment it did not occur to me that when my Lord Jesus had stood in front of Pilate, He wore His beautiful homespun garment instead of a Roman toga. How incongruous that would have been. His clothes hadn't stopped people from listening to Him, that was for sure. How could it be that I still believed those ultra, ultra-suede ladies would only hear what I had to say if I dressed in ultra-suede? I don't know why I didn't reach back in my memories to the coffee bar years and remember I didn't dress in jacket and jeans to get the ear of the kids in the streets. Maybe the fact of the matter was that this women's ministry just wasn't my cup of tea.

I began to believe I should have stuck with the teenagers where my gifts had been tried and trained. How had I gotten into this situation in the first place? It wasn't hard to find the answer. If your husband is a speaker, the public, I found, expects you to be able to follow suit. All sorts of doors of opportunity had opened up to me as soon as I had arrived in the States simply because of Stuart's already well-established ministry. "But I don't *want* to speak to ladies," I had complained to God. He knew I never had liked it when lots of women were compressed together in a confined space. What a row they made, for starters.

Having learned not to be a Jonah and run away from my responsibility to speak to people that I didn't particularly like, I had answered the invitations and gone anyway. *It really doesn't matter that I don't like them very much,* I thought. *After all, they needn't know.* Just like Jonah, I marched into Nineveh (the situation I would like to have marched away from) and talked my heart out, retiring like that same angry prophet to my hill of disdain once the engagement was over. But God apparently used the messages, and I received requests to return.

Then one day I went to Memphis, Tennessee. Verla met me at the airport. She was a speaker and teacher, ran a rescue mission, talked to up-and-outers and down-and-outers, and was totally relaxed with both. She gave me an outsize, uncomfortable feeling in the pit of my conscience the moment I saw her warm touch with the women. We completed our meetings and she was very appreciative of my part, but everything she felt about me came right through her transparent personality. Or maybe she didn't feel like that at all, and it was just that her whole approach and ministry served to rebuke me outright, saying louder than any verbal complaint—"Jill, you are technically a good speaker—*but you do not love these women!*" Being with her was like hearing my slip was showing; it was a different sort of slip this time— the slip of disobedience was hanging down several inches. I knew that love was a conscious decision. I'd learned that from Mary. Also I knew, where these women were concerned, I had definitely decided against love.

The Eternal had long since shown me that love was not just a feeling too big for words, for Jesus had said to His followers, "A new commandment I give unto you, that ye love one another" (John 13:34). I knew that a person couldn't command a feeling. I had come to the conclusion that if love was a command, then I must be able to obey it,

which took it out of the realm of emotions and into the area of actions
. . . loving actions that would involve me in the lives of people I didn't
"feel" I even liked.

Seeing the love of God in action in Verla's life made me want it for
myself. It seemed such a very simple thing to do—reverse my decision,
love the ladies, and then tell the Eternal about it. He was very glad to
hear the news, as He had—unknown to me—thousands more women
for me to meet. From that moment on, the Holy Spirit set about shed-
ding abroad His love for them in my heart.

But did this mean I was to love *all* ladies, or just some? I knew I
would have no problem at all feeling very much at home at the rescue
mission, but what about the ultra, ultra-suede? God could help me
even to love them, I decided, but *that* wasn't the issue—the problem
was would they love *me,* and most important, listen to what I had to
tell them? Once I was on my feet with my Bible open and a prepared
message, I felt fine. It was the before-and-after bit that got to me. The
socializing, and the small talk. The winning of the ladies to myself that
I might win them to Him part. Just as I knew the teens had needed to
like me first in order to listen to what I had to say, I knew the ground
had to be cleared with these sophisticated, clever American women *before* I ever got up behind my security blanket of a pulpit. What I was
like *off* the platform was a question those women had every right to
ask. If they knew my insecurities, if they heard my foolish attempts at
making "classy" conversation, I knew they would dislike me. I groaned
aloud, thinking of the disappointment the women were in for as they
found out there was nothing to me after all.

My companion gave me a strange look. "Is anything wrong?" the
look asked. I wanted to answer, "Yes, me," but less than honestly, I
simply muttered, "I'm sorry to disturb you," and subsided into my
corner of the car again. Stuart had encouraged me to take this particular invitation. He had reminded me of the Eternal's Word that told me
of Paul counting himself in debt to the Jew and the Greek, barbarian
and free. He explained that that meant we all had a debt to pay, that of
sharing the knowledge of salvation with all types of people—and that
included the sophisticated as well as the unsophisticated. Believing it,

I had simply come to pay my debts. The taxi arrived, the meetings came and went, and I returned home just as unsure of everything as I had been when I set out.

In the days that followed, I asked myself if it was simply my Britishness that forbade the crossing of the "class" line—or was my problem just inverted pride? Perhaps it was false humility or a despising of the gifts that others saw in me. I didn't know what was so dreadfully wrong, and so I continued to travel and speak and wonder afterward how on earth I'd had the nerve.

And then one day the Eternal decided it was time to set me free. I was in Coral Gables, Florida, among some of the *nouveau riche* young ladies who populate that classy area of Miami. These certainly could not be classified as the "decorated age" ladies, I decided. In fact they appeared to need no decorating at all. Observing them as they entered the club restaurant where we were dining, I noted each one seemed a beauty in her own lovely right. Sitting at a table with three of the most elegant females, I felt fat, forty, and somewhat futile. Why, oh why, had I come? As my companions ate minute portions of diet dessert and I nervously attacked my pecan pie, I remembered Erma Bombeck saying, "When your dog gives you a strange look when you get out of the shower, it's time to do something about your weight!" It wasn't the dog giving me the strange looks this time, I thought grimly.

I looked around at the beautiful exclusive-like creature who had just made her entrance from an exclusive car into that exclusive place and was about to order some of their exclusive food at a definitely exclusive price. Suddenly and unexpectedly the Eternal inquired of me, "Why do you think everyone is so tense?" I discovered myself in a still point.

"Competition," I replied with sudden comprehension.

"That's right," He answered. It was very, very still in my heart, and so I very distinctly heard the Eternal's next words: "Jill, you'll *never* be competition." That was it—*I was free.* Oh the joy of it. It was true. I could be a big sister to them, a friendly mother to them, an ugly aunt to them. But certainly I could relax knowing I would never threaten one of them. *They were bound to listen to me for the very reason I had believed them bound not to!* What an incredible release!

God had made me just right for my vocation, and that was all that mattered. He had gifted me with ordinary and acceptable good looks. Everywhere I went someone always came up to me and told me I was like their daughter, cousin, or Great Aunt Susan. Now I could see how comfortable that made everybody feel. Why, I was as familiar as family, and instead of being offended by these remarks, conjuring up freaky pictures of Great Aunt Frankenstein Susan, I was able to giggle and be content. I thanked Him for dressing me well enough to hold my own, but not too well to distract or cause envy, freeing me up in that moment of time to wear an outfit twice in a row if I wanted to—and not be trapped in an expensive game of "beat the fashion."

For the first time I was able to be glad for my fine hair, realizing that because it curled so easily, I could always bully it into shape. Instead of majoring on my minors, I began to make a mental list of my best qualities. I did have a sort of pleasant voice (that made a long talk partway enjoyable), and an expressive face (useful for dramatic emphasis), and a metabolism that could be mastered by diet and discipline.

To discover each of us is "just right" in *His eyes* is enough. *He* is the lover of our souls, and to despise the way He has assembled our bodies, dressed our heads with foliage, or arranged our features is to miss the point. To be able to say, "I am free, not to be the 'me' that *I* would choose to be, but the me *He* has already chosen me to be," is freedom indeed.

Set free on the outside, I was about to be set free on the inside as well. Opening the Gospel, I read the words of Zacharias. He prayed for all others, like himself, whose mouths had been closed by fear and doubt—by that dreadful strangling sense of the inadequacy of his body and his faith when faced with God's expectations of him and other people's reactions to him. He was interceding for those of us who would come to know the liberty of a God-confident self-acceptance: "May God grant that we, being delivered out of the hand of our enemies, might *serve him without fear*," I asked, like Zacharias had. God was about to grant me just that.

I had fought this battle for so long, but struggling had brought no victory. I had come across encouraging Scriptures before, but they had not, in the long run, helped. I had prayed earnestly for the fear to be removed and had even sat myself down and been coldly objective about it, telling myself to be reasonable, but that had made no difference—for fear has no reasonable ground.

I had been right on the verge of throwing in the towel altogether, ready to stop accepting invitations, for blind obedience had put me in the position to experience this inordinate fear. I had even tried to analyze my terror into oblivion, digging into my subconscious to find reasons for my anxieties. There was the worry of preparing a talk and not knowing if I had made it interesting enough. For example, I thought of the day I had worked on a study for hours and had confided in Stuart how reticent I was to deliver it. "Why is that?" he inquired.

"The devil is telling me it isn't very interesting," I replied.

"How do you know it's the devil?" he teased with an infuriating grin. I *didn't* know, of course. I just wanted to blame the devil if it bombed.

Then there was the fear of being asked questions I wouldn't be able to answer. "Just say you don't know, if you don't," suggested Stuart with typical male logic. But I certainly hadn't been free enough to do that.

I also struggled with the fear of saying the "wrong" things in the "right" company—a propensity I had already sadly proved. "Adds a bit of spice to the occasion," chaffed my irrepressible mate. On one side of the coin there was the fear of failure—while on the other side there was the fear of success (unlikely though that appeared). Just what might praise or appreciation do to my head and therefore to my sweet relationship with the Lord? "Don't worry about that," Stuart counseled. "The more you're in the spotlight, the more blemishes will be seen." *Oh dear,* I thought, *I don't honestly know if I can be honestly known.*

Letters began to come from editors inviting me to write. Immediately I was suffocated with the fear of writing articles *nobody* would read. Hot on the heels of that anxiety came the worse dread of having people read them and rip them apart doctrinally, or write nasty letters to the editor that *everybody* would read. Surely in the light—or I should say "dark"—of all this, the obvious solution was to stay home and do the things on the home front that I *knew* I could do.

But now as I had taken time out to meet with and listen to God in the still point, and with the memory of Coral Gables fresh in my mind, the Eternal again applied His Word to my heart. He reminded me of some of the deliverances He had already given me. The way He had overcome the fear of losing friends, of witnessing of my faith, of being attacked on the back streets of Liverpool. The fear of something happening to the children or to Stuart and the horror of rejection and death.

He had dealt with the apprehension of adjusting to our new environment and the awful fear of flying. He had visited me with the written Word as He had visited Zacharias with the Living Word; and it had proved to be sweeter than honey, finer than gold, more precious than rubies. Even my fearful obediences had brought me great reward. They had led to marvelous adventures that I wouldn't have missed for anything. But now I knew that the promise to serve Him *without fear* was for *me* and had everything to do with the ultra-suede ladies.

As I knelt the Father dressed my spirit with an incredibly tender anticipation of heavenly delight, and I told the Lord Jesus how much I loved Him for it all—He who must have been tempted to be afraid so many, many times. He had refused to doubt His Father's faithfulness to Him. He could have feared Mary wouldn't bear Him or Joseph wouldn't guard Him, the angel wouldn't announce Him or the innkeeper wouldn't provide for Him. He could have stayed home with His Father because He dreaded the cross beams of a tree, some iron nails, and a soldier's hammer. He could have decided not to be a suffering servant for fear what He went through wouldn't make any difference. But He came anyway and didn't shudder at the oblivion of the womb, the rejection of the world, or the agony of the cross—because He feared His Father first. *The fear of God, rather than the fear of man, was the key.* Fear in the sense of reverent trust, coupled with hatred of sin.

Shuffling through my invitations with a quickening excitement, I chose three of the most challenging I had ever been given and wrote an eager acceptance. Surprised by peace and with an incredible new hope, I breathed—West Point, Princeton, Washington—ultra, ultra-suede ladies . . . here we come! And as I went it was with the prayer of Psalm 19 uppermost in my thinking.

> Let the words of my mouth, and the meditation of my heart, be acceptable *in thy sight,* O Lord, my *strength,* and my *redeemer!* (Psalm 19:14 KJV, italics added)

As I stood on platforms here and there, and felt wooden planks or shiny bricks underneath my feet, I somehow knew I would begin to feel another substance undergirding my obediences—"my Rock." That new confidence in my Redeemer's promises would begin to work in me a new sense of well-being with myself.

When I got to Washington, I noticed fashions must have changed. I couldn't see any ultra-suede around. Then I looked a little closer and found it was there all the time. It wasn't even ultra-suede, but ultra, ultra, ultra. At last I was seeing the people in it, and they, I found, were just like everyone else. As I sought to have words from the Eternal that were *acceptable in His sight,* I found *they accepted them too.* I could even table-hop around the exclusive restaurants, chat about anything or nothing at the reception, and enjoy it all. What a life.

My ministry took on a new swing—an exuberance, a depth of satisfaction and sureness I'd never known before. When I got to a huge convention and found a little man hired to make room keys sitting in the middle of the lobby, I laughed uproariously. Only women would need to hire a man to do *that,* I reckoned with tender appreciation. Flying outside to catch a plane to the next assignment, I smiled at the jumble of cars and my frantic hostess running around like a scalded cat—she couldn't remember where she'd parked. I was reminded of my husband's quip, "Women don't park cars; they abandon them." The next time some dear little blue-haired ladies in tennis shoes came and whispered in my ear, "We couldn't hear you," and I asked, "Where were you sitting?" and they answered me, "On the back row and we're all deaf you know," I found a sweet warmth and loving concern instead of the old irritation as I patiently suggested they sit on the front row next time.

It was all different. Women were everywhere. In my head and in my heart, in my plans and in my thinking, in my schedules and spare moments, on the phone and in my car, at the restaurant, and at tennis, in my tears and in my laughter—they were part of me and I was part and parcel of them. And I was *glad, glad, glad*—we were women together!

To Be a Friend: Application and Journal

. . . .

1. What category of person do you find it hard to relate to? Why?

Do you find that most of your friends are married or most are single (whichever you are)? What are some practical things you can do to bridge the gap with people you know?

2. As a woman made in God's image, you are honestly known by Him. If Christ is your Savior, you are fully accepted by Him (though sin can hinder that relationship). When is that difficult for you to believe? How would your life be different if you were honestly known by *people?*

3. Do you have a hard time loving women? In what areas do you need to make a decision to love or to enjoy "being women together" with others?

4. How much control does fear have over you? (Don't answer that too quickly.) How can fear of God cast out fear of people?

. . . .

For Action:
Invite someone outside your normal friendship category to have dinner at your house. If that is too awkward, ask her to meet you for coffee at a restaurant that will be comfortable for both of you.
. . . .

Chapter Eleven

Prayer Friends

The first recollection I have of someone praying for me goes back to my childhood.

I was playing cards with my mother. My sister was at school, but I was sick and had stayed home from kindergarten. The radio played quietly in the background. My mother had tucked me up in a rug, and I was warm and comfortable by the coal fire in our morning room—a cozy place where we ate and played. It was Second World War time in Britain and the radio was not allowed to be turned off—by order of the government. There was no television in those days, so that little brown box was our lifeline to crucial news bulletins from Winston Churchill and the war cabinet. My father was away serving in the R.A.F., and like thousands of others' mothers, mine went about her daily doings with as much composure as possible so as not to panic her children.

We were in the middle of a game—I remember distinctly having two queens, a king, a two, and a three in my hand, and I was chattering away—when the emergency radio signal sounded. "Shhh!" my mother said. I shushed. The message was quite urgent. We were instructed to prepare for "the invasion." Those living along the coastline (we lived in the port city of Liverpool) were advised to pack a small case and have it ready by the front door—just in case.

"In case of what?" I asked my mother, my heart beginning to race as I watched her anxious eyes.

"Just in case" she replied—"Just in case." Then she prayed. She didn't pray out loud, but she closed her eyes and got hold of my small hand that still clutched the cards we had been playing with, and her lips moved. I knew she was praying for my sister and me. My small heart still pounded even though somehow I knew that that prayer my mother prayed that day was supposed to help me. She got up and went away to pack, and I looked into the warm coals and wondered what that long word "invasion" meant for us. Would our lives ever be the same again? Somehow I knew it would be all right in the end because my daddy was in the R.A.F. and I knew our air force was keeping us all safe!

The next weeks were very scary. Every time I passed the front door I saw those three suitcases standing there reminding me of that dreaded word "invasion." The radio kept interrupting its programming so we could keep up with the *Battle of Britain* that was going on. At night we spent time in the underground "dug out" bomb shelter my dad had made for us in our garden. It was hard to sleep. When a big bomb would fall with an incredible "boom," my mother would get hold of our hands, close her eyes—and her lips would move again. Shirley and I knew what she was doing. Once I closed my eyes and moved my lips too. Mother had told me about Jesus and I knew who to talk to. I asked Him pretty straightforward things like "Please keep Daddy safe" or "Please stop the war."

One day Winston Churchill asked everyone who could to stay home from work. We were to go to church and pray for our troops who were trapped at a place called Dunkirk. They couldn't get home because the sea was behind them and the enemy was in front of them.

My mother dressed us in our best clothes, and we walked to the nearest church. My sister and I had never been to church, so I was excited. But when we arrived, we couldn't get in because it was full. Hundreds of people were just kneeling down praying in the street. I looked at my mother. She nodded to us, so we knelt down right there on the hard pavement and prayed. She kept hold of our hands, and somehow the thought came to me in childish terms, "There's power in this." And there was! England brought to its knees in its extremity sought God, and in His grace He heard and answered corporate prayer and eventually delivered us. As we walked home again, I remember feeling very close to my mother and sister—closer than before we'd prayed together—and I knew that business of praying had a lot to do with it!

So all those years ago I learned a vital lesson. Prayer is a place where people draw closer to each other, and prayer is a place where true friends are born! In fact, prayer is a place where even relatives, like a mother and daughter, can become closer friends.

Over the years since those turbulent, dangerous days, I have found the same principle pertains. We have an enemy of our souls called Satan, and he would declare war on us and ours and attack us whenever he can. He would mount an invasion when we're weak and vulnerable and drop bombs all over our lives! He is out to destroy us all. But we can reach out and take the hand of whoever is nearest to us and stand against him in the name of Jesus, our Captain and Savior. We can pray! Whenever we do we will experience and know a closeness with those we pray with that we didn't know before—it's called "prayer friendship"!

Many of my dearest friendships have been birthed in such prayer. I owe much to Janet—the girl in the hospital who led me to Christ. One of the main things she did for me was pray for me and with me. I will never forget her asking me these questions: "Do you need Jesus, Jill? Do you want Him? Will you accept Him?" "Yes," I answered simply. "Then we need to pray," she said. She got hold of my hand, like my mother had—right there in the hospital ward—and shut her eyes! I felt somewhat self-conscious. What would happen if anyone saw us? But the touch of her hand brought back sharp memories of my mother's hand that dark day during the Battle of Britain, and I was reminded of the spiritual intimacy that prayer invites us to enjoy.

Janet was my spiritual mother and became my committed prayer friend. I used to look forward to praying with Janet—and later with others that I had the privilege of leading to Christ. I have learned to enjoy all aspects of the friendships God has given me, but I have realized that praying together deepens, cleanses, strengthens, and develops relationships more than any other activity we may enjoy together. This is especially true when we pray about mutual ministry.

The story is told of a farmer who lost his small boy in the tall grain during wheat harvest. He and his wife searched frantically, calling out the child's name, but at the end of the day they still hadn't found him. At dawn the entire village assembled in the farmer's yard. Stretching out in a long line right along one entire side of the grain field, they joined hands and began to walk forward together. About three-fourths of the way through the field they found the little boy's body. The child was dead. Lifting his little boy in his arms, the father cried out, "Oh, if we had only joined hands sooner!" There are many lost people in this world. If we would only join hands and walk forward together in the ministry of prayer, we stand a good chance of finding the lost ones.

Early on in my faith adventure I was introduced to this concept of meeting together with prayer friends. At Cambridge University there was a daily prayer meeting during lunch hour. Shortly after coming to Christ, I was taken along to it by a friend. The church was packed with black-gowned undergraduates. The time flew by. Someone would give five minutes of information about an area of the world, and we would break into small groups. Joining hands, we earnestly "walked through the wheat field together."

"Bless Africa," I remember intoning fervently when my turn came.

"Which part of Africa?" my friend inquired in my ear. "Which missionary are you praying for, and what are the difficulties that missionary faces? What about their family—their health?" I realized in a hurry that "bless Africa" was not going to do it! That particular prayer friend finished up serving the Lord in an East African hospital, and we have continued praying for each other for more than forty years.

Through this I discovered a very exciting thing. When you can't spend time with a friend in person, you can always spend time with her in prayer! All I have to do is shut my eyes and I'm in East Africa, right in the hospital by my friend's side. I can talk to the Lord about all the difficulties she faces, the fact that there's not enough medicine or equipment—or the struggle the missionaries face against the people's pagan beliefs. I can talk to Jesus about tiredness that is the result of age, heat, or a diet lacking in nutrients. It's a fantastic way to be a friend in need!

Ministry friends are the sort of friends that I would probably never go shopping or play tennis with if we were living on the same continent, but they are my precious "ministry friends." Our love for each other has been nurtured in the fertile field of prayer.

As I began to be invited around the globe, I realized I needed a prayer team myself. Tentatively, I invited our women's ministry board at church to pray about it. A few weeks later, six women told me the Lord had impressed it upon them to "go with me" on my travels in prayer. Along with my dear secretary of more than twenty-three years, these women have faithfully packed their prayer bags and come along!

Travel is a lot of fun, a lot of trouble, tiring, boring, exciting, taxing, challenging, and an education. It shows you who you are, who other people are, and who God is! To travel to exotic, dirty, beautiful, terrible, faraway places may sound like a dream to some, but it can swiftly turn into a nightmare without prayer support. These women have traveled everywhere with me. They committed to pray as the invitations to speak and travel began to accelerate. They have journeyed to Africa, Asia, Europe, the Middle East. These are my prayer friends!

Many times on my return, I have told how difficult a situation had been—transport breaking down, extreme climates zapping my strength, a bad back playing up—and my prayer friends smile knowingly. The Holy Spirit had "told" them all about it. I learned never to shortchange what the Holy Spirit did before I got home again.

One time I was traveling to India from Northern Ireland. When I arrived, my luggage—including all my notes for my lectures—was lost. As I began to explain my problem to the airport official, I discovered I had lost my voice completely. So now I had no notes and no voice. We traveled up country for a day to my first speaking engagement, but when we arrived at the campsite no one was there. So now I had no luggage, notes, voice, or conference! The plague had broken out in this very town, and there had been a mass exodus of doctors, patients, and people from the entire region. We joined it!

During the next three weeks one dilemma after another happened. I never did get my luggage or my notes, and my voice only partially returned, but I would say I saw more people touched and changed by God during that time in India than I had for a long, long time. Of course I knew why. My faithful "soldiers" were doing battle on the home front as they learned of the problems. Such circumstances force you onto your knees and into His arms. And He was nudging my friends to pray for me at just the right time and in just the right way. There were far too many "coincidences" to warrant mere circumstance being the reason for things falling into place along the way.

I have discovered prayer friends communicate on a very deep level. Telling your highest hopes and deepest fears means exposing your failures in a safe place—knowing confidences will be kept and told to no one but the Lord. Praying for someone at a deep level means you pick up conversation at the same level when you meet face-to-face. Friendship grown on your knees blossoms on your feet. Prayer gives you great confidence that you can really do something significant for your friends. Part of friendship is giving, and what better gift than the gift of prayer!

The deepest bonds of friendship with other women have been forged for me in the fires of affliction. As trouble came to one of our children, I flew to my prayer team. I well remember their concerned, anxious faces as I poured out my pain. "I can't pray," I said.

"You don't need to," they assured me. "That's what we're here for!" From that moment on for a long time these women, along with many others, interceded for our family. The group met once a week. If I was traveling, it didn't matter—they met anyway. Sometimes I had to get up in front of thousands of people and talk about faith when I felt I wasn't trusting God at all. Or I needed to testify to the companionship of the Lord and I felt as though I was terribly alone in an empty universe, when suddenly I would sense a deep calm enveloping me and I was trusting again. I knew why. My prayer friends were back home being faithful! Now that our personal crisis is over, we have time to pray for each other when we meet. All of us have ongoing pain and problems, and we grasp each other's troubles and lay them at the feet of Him who died and rose again for us. Prayer friends are such a gift from God!

Ministry is a grand place to make and cultivate friends. God has given me sweet friends in the publishing world as books have been conceived, brought to birth, and sent out to make me new friends I will probably never meet face-to-face. Friends have been made across the world in relief and development work as I have gone to put my personal "drop in the bucket" of the appalling need around the world. One of the greatest times for me was taking ten women to Croatia for a relief organization—at the height of the war in Bosnia. It does something for friendship when you join hands to walk through that particular wheat field together. We handed out a lot of clothes on that trip. We served meals, gave a hand wherever we could, and spoke in many churches. We cried together, listened together, and most of all prayed together. It was those times in intercession that cemented our team in friendship.

Speakers on the same platform have become some of my closest friends too. Prominent speakers and little-known teachers, committee members and women who have gone out on a limb to invite me to come for the first time to their church or mission field, have bonded as we've put our combined gifts together for Him. The amazing thing about ministry friends is you don't even have to speak the same language for bonds to form. I have friends in Bulgaria, Cambodia, Thailand, Indonesia, Hungary, and Palestine—and so many, many more places. We have nothing in common but Jesus, and yet that is more than enough for an ongoing basis of friendship through ministry.

The bonding element, of course, is the Holy Spirit. We have the same faith in a crucified, risen Lord and a combined mission to tell the world about Him—together! To weep and laugh together, plan and serve together, travel or stay put together, lead or follow together—minister together and pray together.

Not long ago my small granddaughter was sitting next to me on a plane. It was bumpy and her eyes grew wide with concern. We were playing cards. I put my hand down and got hold of her small fist—still clutching her hand full of cards. I shut my eyes, and my lips moved. I opened my eyes and looked at her. Yes, she, like I many years ago, knew exactly what I was doing. She smiled at me—a grateful smile— and we went back to our game. What a heritage is mine to pass on to the next generations. That little girl and I are destined to become the greatest of friends!

To Be a Friend: Application and Journal
....

1. What memories do you have of other people praying for you?

2. With which of your friends or relatives do you have a "prayer friendship"? What individuals—or which groups—might come alongside you in mutual prayer?

3. Many friendships are born in ministry. Are you part of a group of people with similar interests (a college class, Sunday school class, ministry group, etc.) that has other people you might "connect" with? How can you deepen such relationships?

4. Whom do you know who needs prayer? Why? (To protect their privacy, do not write intensely personal needs here.) Are there physical needs in their lives in which you might *be* an answer to prayer?

. . . .

For Action:
Give a "third-party compliment": Tell two other people something you appreciate about a friend or partner in ministry that both of them know. Then tell God how much you appreciate that friend.

. . . .

Chapter Twelve

....

Judy

....

$\mathcal{S}$he is my daughter—born Judith Margaret Briscoe on June 17, 1961. She is my friend—miracle of miracles—closer than any peer, dearer than any woman in my life. She is our middle child with a beloved brother on either side.

Born as her dad and mum had just started their life career in missions, she knew nothing else but a God-centered environment from her earliest days. Our home was not an oasis *from* ministry but rather an oasis *of* ministry. I can see in my mind's eye Judy's turquoise "carry cot" (a useful little bed with handles we could put on the backseat of a car) sitting in the middle of the tiny living room in our home at mission headquarters. Judy—age six months—lay smiling and kicking away. Children from the farms and villages around sat on the floor around the cot watching and listening to her and occasionally watching and listening to me as I led songs on my guitar and told Bible stories. This was Sunday school—for David, Judy, and later Peter, and their little friends. Children who lived within walking distance from our home and who were by and large unchurched made up our small congregation. These tiny tots were to be our children's friends and schoolmates.

When the time came to go to the village school, Judy and about twelve other kids from the mission and the vicinity piled into our minibus and I drove them down the narrow, winding country lanes to the one-room schoolhouse in a sleepy little English village called Over Kellet. Big school began at age four in England. I remember my daughter coming home one day very upset. Her older brother David had been asked by his teacher if he would like to sing. "No," he replied adamantly. "Then go and stand in the corner," the schoolmarm commanded. Knowing all the children could see and hear what was going on, Judy watched aghast as David was banished to the corner, where he sat on a little wooden stool with his face to the wall for the entire music period.

"It's no fair!" my four year old sobbed inconsolably that evening. "The teacher asked him if he wanted to sing, and he said no! So why did she ask him?" At the tender age of four Judy could sense that life was "no fair," and she objected loudly and bitterly.

Thirty years later Judy became her brother's advocate and confidant as David experienced the bitter unfairness of life lived in a fallen environment. As she walked through a particularly deep valley with her dearly loved big brother, I could hear a little sister's voice from the past complaining loudly and loyally "It's no fair." Her relationship with David had grown up into love. Together they weathered the storm; together they stood firm for God and rightness.

Judy's friendship with her younger brother is a fiercely guarded one too. Peter, while in seminary, recommended that his professors consider his big sister, Judy, for a place on the teaching faculty. Judy interviewed and was accepted. Brother affirmed and prayed for his sister in her gift and calling, and later Judy proudly affirms and prays for her younger brother as he leads a large and vibrant church. What joy to see our children close ranks when the enemies have come against one or another of them and have found them all standing for each other and for God's truth in a crooked and perverse world.

Fellowship is another word for friendship—but friendship with a difference. The friendships that are shared as each is a friend of God have indestructible qualities to them. I have a theory that the closer friend we become with the Lord, the closer we will become to each other. It has certainly been so in our family, particularly regarding Judy's and my friendship as well as Judy's and Stuart's. This mother-father-daughter friendship, if I may coin a phrase, has brought such joy to us it's hard to talk about. The joy I feel when I watch Stuart lying on the bed, phone to his ear, sharing Judy's chatter and engaging her in both fun and serious verbal exchange warms my heart and sets my soul a-dancing. We generally fight over the phone whenever any of our kids call us, yet gain great satisfaction watching each other "win" the race to talk and listen first.

In our family one element of friendship is this free flow of ideas: feeling safe enough to talk through the deep waters, recreate in the shallow streams, and challenge each other with the new things each is learning without fear of feeling silly or irrelevant.

Teenage years gave Judy and me the opportunity to use the fertile soil of conversation to explain each to the other and create a safe place to grow. I had to learn I needed to be available when she was—not when I was. That was the first lesson. Usually that turned out to be about 11:00 P.M. to 1:00 A.M. Not my best hours—but that was when Judy was at her brightest and most communicative, and I discovered I'd better be there if I was to grow our relationship to maturity. It was from these late-night "tell all" talk times that I learned what to pray about. My prayer life took a leap forward when I had teenagers, especially a teenage daughter.

The friendship that Judy and I enjoy is born out of togetherness; it has also been born out of prayer and nurtured in prayer. It is based on our individual commitment to pray for each other as a matter of course all day every day. This has been our joint commitment to each other. The very best thing you can ever do for a friend is pray for her. This began for me when Judy was a baby and developed as she grew old enough to accept Christ. The greatest bond is that of belief. What a joy I was to experience as I led Judy to the Jesus I loved to distraction and served as best I knew how.

The days at the youth mission were busy beyond imagining. My husband traveled extensively, and I tried to do the woman's part of the ministry equation by being mom and dad at home, making life "fun" while I pulled my weight in the youth center. We—three kids and I—played the lonely months away, till Daddy got home again. One day, busy at my baking board, I heard my six, four, and two year olds scrapping over territory in the playroom. Suddenly Judy appeared, eyes bright, with red in her cheeks, small arms straining to encircle all her worldly goods. After all, she was the only girl in the family and had to carry everything everywhere every time she moved. She had discovered it was the only "safe" way to keep control.

It was time to clear up for supper, and I called to the kids to start to pick up, pack up, and stack up the merry mess they'd made. Judy stood still at the edge of my baking board solemnly considering the command. Then she took my breath away by asking, "If I ask Jesus into my heart, will He want me to put my toys all away when you tell me to?"

"Yes, darling," I replied promptly, "the Lord Jesus would want you to obey Mommy."

"Then I won't ask Him into my heart," she replied firmly and, leaving my baking board, headed back to the playroom. Startled, I scolded myself for answering an incredibly important question too glibly. Why hadn't I hauled her into the kingdom, then told her all about the "small print" after it was done? To my relief my little girl reappeared, still clutching everything to her bosom, and announced in a determined way, "It's all right—I'll put my toys away." That said it all. She understood that asking Jesus into one's heart equaled "a long obedience in the same direction" and was ready for the hike.

Without waiting to wash the teatime dough from my fingers, I took Judy's hand. In front of her two interested brothers I knelt down with my "tiny best friend" and led her to the Jesus she and I were going to love and serve together.

Joy in Heaven—angels singing—
light and laughter, church bells ringing.

A little sinner had been led by a bigger sinner right up to a cross beam to meet our Savior. Glory! So the underpinnings of the very deepest of friendships was laid.

I had many more years ahead of me to learn how vital it is to nurture one's daughter's friendship with God, if a mother hopes to nurture her friendship with her. When Judy was nine, God moved us thousands of miles over the Atlantic to Elmbrook Church. Stuart sent word from America that I needed to go and meet the church fellowship in Brookfield, Wisconsin, that had called us to pastor the congregation. I was to be away three weeks. During this time Judy, Dave, and Pete were to be cared for by a wonderful girl who lived with us (a nurse). Almost as soon as we arrived in America for the visit, Judy had a nasty accident, putting her hand and arm through a window and severing the tendon in her wrist right through. Complications arose, and Judy found herself alone in a sterile ward in a big English hospital where visitors were allowed only twice a week. She tells me that something happened in the darkness one night when a young girl frightened and lonely called out to her heavenly Friend and Savior Jesus to come and help her. God gladly answered that little girl's prayer and made His presence felt. Now she knew it would be all right. In the measure in which both Judy and I have nurtured our dependence on this present God whenever we have needed Him, we have found we have drawn closer to each other too. If either of us stops looking to God and starts relying first and foremost on the other, our friendship atrophies.

But how would I grow our friendship during the turbulent teen years in America? I worried. What sort of relationship would develop as we wrestled through the issues of self-worth, independence, discipline, and communication—and all in a foreign culture where I'd never read the rule book? What if either of us stopped growing in God—would our friendship stop too?

As we hit the stretching years I canceled out of some ministry commitments and replaced them with "Judy" commitments, writing in "us time" in an overscheduled life. We joined a racquetball club and played together once a week after school. I learned to sit up later and later because that's when *she* wanted to "gab" and talk about the things *she* wanted to talk about, not the things I was interested in. We tried to navigate the teenage icebergs the devil steered us toward.

I began the incredible lesson of role reversal as young wisdom countered my mother fears and worries. For instance, I worried about her boyfriends. "You have to pray all my mistakes will be small ones," she advised. Wise words! I was demanding "no mistakes," but she countered with "That's not fair—you made yours. Let me make mine, Mom, but let's pray they won't be 'life threatening.'"

One night we talked long and late about the "ideal husband." A large poster of Robert Redford smiled down at us from the back of Judy's bedroom door. "I'd like one like that—but a Christian," she said. We laughed.

"Well now, let's ask Him—there's no harm in that," I said. And so we did. Is it our imagination (and that of many others) that Greg, Judy's husband, looks not a little like Mr. Redford himself? I think not.

I knew new lessons of friendship were pending as Judy met and fell in love with Greg Golz while studying at Wheaton College. How would she and I make room for the man of her prayers? We knew how much she wanted the family to love him, and I realized I needed to respond to that unspoken request and begin to be a friend to my future son-in-law. I prayed about it. *How did one do this?* I wondered. I decided to take the bull by the horns and talk to him, so I took him out to breakfast.

He was shy, and I'm sure he wondered why this strange, intense woman wanted to ply him with stacks of pancakes at some unearthly hour of the morning. As he began to relax, I said, "Greg, I know Judy usually tells her boyfriends—if she senses they're getting serious—that if they have thought of anything permanent, she needs them to know she would not respond unless they promise to have her mother come and live with them when she's old and infirm." He looked up at me not a little startled, and I smiled and said, "Greg, I promise you I won't be doing that." We laughed together, and the moment passed, paving the way for us to begin appreciating and understanding each other and above all having fun. What a friend our son-in-law has become to us. There is no question in my mind that that one thing has been a big reason my friendship with Judy is closer than ever today.

As Judy married and I warned her she must always turn first to Greg before she picked up the phone to me, she answered absent-mindedly, "Of course, Mom." However, it was only a short time after this conversation we received a tearful call in the early hours of the morning. "We've had a fight," Judy sobbed.

Everything in me wanted to run down the telephone line with a hammer in my hand—but with a supreme effort I managed to ask, "Does Greg know you're calling me? Because if he doesn't, I won't talk to you."

"Of course he knows," she sobbed, "he told me to. He said, 'I don't know what's the matter with you, Judy—maybe your mother can sort you out!'"

Trying to respect boundaries has stopped me competing for Judy's friendship with her husband, or anyone else, for that matter.

Another element of the wonderful relationship we have is that of shared service. From the earliest days I have involved the children in our mission. All the kids came with me to visit neighbors as I tried to start a women's Bible study. They took it for granted they would sleep in sleeping bags when teenagers in trouble came to live with us and needed their beds. They watched young adults come off drugs and saw changed lives, as well as noting the lessons to be learned as they observed young lives that were marred and spoiled and lost through the consequences of their own bad choices. They were part and parcel of a ministry home, and it was exciting, bringing grand adventure and drawing us all close to one another.

As Judy grew up in America enjoying a vibrant and exciting youth experience at church, I began to get invitations to travel and speak to women's groups. I took Judy—age fifteen—and her close friend Kerrie with me to sing. We traveled together by car or air. This had its moments. Both girls invariably disappeared to the bathroom just as we were boarding the plane, giving me fits. But what a trip! Now my nights got even later, since two teenagers giggle and chatter a lot later into the night than one teenager. We got to take mother/daughter meetings and whole weekends. The girls began to help their peers at these events, and God gave them opportunities to grow and stretch in their faith walk. Something about serving Jesus together does wonders for your friendships. It's great to play and laugh—to enjoy sports and movies, racquetball and clothes shopping (and we do!)—but there's nothing quite like talking about Christ with each other and with others. I remember feeling a pang on Judy's wedding day thinking those wonderful days were over. Little did I know what was to be just around the corner of tomorrow.

After Judy and Greg's wedding, they settled down to graduate school. Greg was at Northwestern finishing up an MBA, and Judy was waitressing until he finished and she could start her Ph.D. work in New York.

I was preparing to visit Australia to take women's conventions across the country. "You should take someone with you," my husband said.

Talking to Judy that evening on the phone, I asked her, "Who do you think I should invite to come with me?"

Judy shouted over her shoulder to her brand-new husband, "Greg, Mom's going to Australia and needs someone as a traveling companion. Can you think of anyone?"

"How about you?" I heard Greg call back. Judy was slightly put out—they had only just been married a few months—but she decided after much thought she'd come. Greg was heading up for six weeks of heavy studies and could well do with the peace and quiet. And so we prepared to go to Australia for five weeks of ministry.

About two weeks before we were due to leave, my back went out. *Never mind,* I thought, *Judy will help me with my baggage*—I'll be all right. But I wasn't all right—I was as all wrong as I could be. Sitting on the plane for that excruciating long flight, I tried to get up to go to the restroom and discovered my lower back had locked into place. As I struggled to get out of my seat, my muscles went into spasm, and I fell back gasping. Judy looked at me in horror. "Don't do this to me, Mother," she said. But it was done. We looked at each other. I knew from experience that it would be six weeks before I would fully mend and that pain was to be the order of the day from then on.

The welcoming committee's smiles faded as they watched the

stewardess wheel me into the terminal. This was not on their agenda. That night, with me in acute pain, Judy and I talked it over. "You'll have to help me, Judy."

"How?" she asked apprehensively.

"You'll have to take some of the meetings," I replied.

"Mom, I've only spoken to the church youth group—"

"What about?" I asked with interest.

"Anxiety," she said with a grin.

"Great," I answered. "What better topic!"

She looked at me for a long time and said, "Mom, I can't remember one word of my talk—I'm too anxious!"

"Yes, you can," I said desperately. "Come on—we're not going to sleep tonight until you remember something. Anyway what with jet lag and back pain we can't sleep anyway—we can get that talk together." And so Judy's and my ministry began.

The first day of the convention, thousands of women were gathered together. I took the first meeting sitting down and in lots of trouble. I was wet through with the effort when it was over. Meanwhile Judy was pacing up and down outside like a caged lion. During the break women were coming up to her and telling her what a wonderful speaker her mother was. She didn't need to hear that at that particular moment and had in fact sat listening to me for a while praying, "Lord, don't let her be *too* good." She found a quiet spot away from all of us and prayed, "Lord, I can't do this—I'm not my mother—help me." Opening her Bible she found a verse that spoke directly to her. She can't even remember what or where it was, but in effect it told her that everyone has a gift and not one is without significance.

"You have something to say that your Mother could never say, Judy," it seemed like the Lord told her, "and after all, who better than you to talk about anxiety?" She smiled at the Lord and took on the challenge—as she has done all of her life—telling her fears to all those women, who, as you can imagine, took her right to their hearts. Which of us would not identify with her dilemma?

Somewhere on that trip a great heavenly affirmation and sense of joy flooded her life as she sensed God confirming her speaking gifts. I believe that inner joy is our soul sensing His pleasure as He sees us find our gifts and calling.

We put together our first seminar in Australia sharing the platform and teaching about mother/daughter relationships from the book of Ruth. Much later that material found its way into the first of our three books, *Space to Breathe, Room to Grow.*

How can I tell of the deep, exhilarating joy of hundreds of shared meetings over these last fifteen years? Not long ago our hostess picked us up at the airport and we sat in the back of the car, both of us talking at the same time, laughing and giggling and celebrating our time together in such exuberance, the lady who was driving asked, "Whenever did you last see each other?"

"Two days ago," Judy replied at once.

There was silence from the front seat and then a sad comment: "I wish—I wish my daughter and I were such good friends."

Such comments remind us to be sensitive to others' sadness in this area and not to be exclusive and selfish when we're together in a group.

Judy now has a ministry of her own—teaching at Trinity International University in Chicago and speaking around the country. But we still schedule at least six meetings a year together. There is a power, we have discovered, in sharing our friendship in ministry to other women, and there is always blessing to us.

Friendship that shuts others out instead of inviting them in will never grow. In fact, friendship must have open arms to others to really develop itself. This lesson has been brought home to me since three precious little grandchildren have added their considerable presence to the equation of Judy's and my friendship. What a gift to be invited to stay with Judy and Greg for the days immediately following their children's births.

Drew decided to arrive in the middle of a deep freeze. The evening he was brought home the boiler went out in the middle of the night. The temperature was well below zero, and here were Judy and Drew and me huddled under mountains of blankets, our breath frosty— while Greg searched desperately for a neighbor who could help him fix the problem. It was a "no fair" thing to happen—but God provided an expert who lived just down the street to help.

What a miracle of joy these three little boys are to us. Yet greater is the joy than even their births to pick up the phone (I just beat Stuart to the draw) and to hear Judy's excited voice telling us, "Mom and Dad, Drew's just accepted Jesus with me." He was four years of age—just like his mommy. And so the heritage goes on—and on—and on. Now grandmother and mother can learn different lessons in the school of friendship as together we invest for God in these small lives.

I'm still growing in many areas of my friendship with my children. I'm learning that relinquishment of control doesn't equal relinquishment of relationship. In fact, holding my friendship "lightly not tightly" gives me back my children's companionship. There's a fine line between grandparenting and grand-baby-sitting that has to be prayed about and talked through with each of our kids—as each vary in styles of parenting. It's hard to talk deeply and personally about these issues with those you love the most for fear of making matters worse—but it must be done if deeply held adult friendships are to be kept fresh and new and *growing*.

My Judy is the sun, moon, and stars to me—but she is not a god. God must be the God of our friendship, and we must never make our relationship God—for that is idolatry. Above all, our friendship must stay on its knees, for that's where it belongs. Each day I thank the Lord Jesus for His cross that made us sisters, and for His grace that rules our lives from the throne. "If God be for us, who can be against us?"

To Be a Friend: Application and Journal

....

1. What are the strengths in your current relationship with your daughter? (If you do not have a daughter, think of another younger relative or a student or protégée.)

2. What could you do better? How can you develop your relationship into a partnership, or how can you prepare for the day when that will be appropriate? How can you use your partnership to encourage others?

3. What steps have you taken recently either to relinquish control or to affirm your daughter's gifts? What steps do you need to take?

4. How can you encourage each other to grow closer to God? Be practical and specific.

. . . .

For Action:
Give your daughter a handmade book of coupons. If your daughter is
an adult, it could include one evening of free baby-sitting
(or one collect call), one favorite story of yours—her choice—
that you'll never tell again, one backrub, a reusable hug coupon,
and a hand-delivered batch of her favorite childhood cookies.

. . . .